Black to Play

Classical Defenses

Eric Schiller

and Win

Chess Digest, Inc

D1438445

Author: Eric Schiller

Manuscript preparation: M.L. Rantala for Chessworks Unlimited

Typeset in Tilburg Laserfont.

Cover: Elaine Smith

Proofreading: John Hall, Ken Smith, and David Sewell

Publisher: Chess Digest, Inc., 1601 Tantor, Dallas, Texas, 75229.

Send the publisher $2 for the New Chess Guide that catalogs every book and chess item for general sale in the United States. You are given publishers, page counts, notation, diagram numbers, colors, and sizes of each item along with numerous pictures. Also included is a free Chess Improvement Course for beginners up through Master level.

Table of Contents

Introduction

Chess is a game which is primarily played for fun. But like many activities, it requires a certain investment of time and energy to acquire the skills which will allow one to play competitively. After all, it is no fun to lose all the time! After learning the basic rules of chess, there are a number of fundamental principles and tactical ideas which must be learned. These can be divided into the three stages of the game: opening, middlegame, and endgame. Assuming that the basics have already been mastered, the opening can be handled without too much difficulty. Middlegame expertise comes primarily as a result of experience, and the thorough study of grandmaster games. The endgame is one of the most important aspects of chess play, and requires considerable study.

Now why would a book on an opening repertoire start out by claiming that the endgame and the middlegame are more important areas of study? The answer is that chessplayers, and American chessplayers especially, place far too much emphasis on trying to obtain a significant advantage in the opening, especially with White. There is a notion that if enough material is absorbed, often by sheer memorization, that victories will pile up without effort. By luring an opponent into some opening trap, highly unorthodox opening or prepared line, a full point can be picked up before lunch.

That is a wrongheaded approach which will never lead to success as a chessplayer. There are a number of reasons for this. One consequence of that approach is the failure to study games by great players How does that follow from the choice of openings? It is really quite simple. Frankly, almost all chessplayers tend to study games primarily in the opening lines they play. So if one chooses to play some offbeat line like the Grimswold Gambit, one is hardly likely to come accross many examples by grandmasters. Thus one winds up studying games by players of much lower caliber, and the middlegame and endgames will be of lower quality in most cases.

An ideal first opening repertoire is a selection of lines which are on the one hand seen in the praxis of great players, but at the same time do not require the memorization of a lot of variations. Furthermore, the lines should be somewhat tactically oriented, not demanding a deep appreciation of strategically complex themes. But this is not achievable, for the simple reason that the great players often favor inappropriate lines, especially in modern tournament play. So some compromises are required.

The first compromise is a remarkably mild one. Instead of concentrating on the repertoires of modern champions, we consider the openings used by classical heroes of the 20th century. We find that these players often chose lines which have been relegated to the attic of modern opening theory. These variations faded from popularity because after a number of years opponents eventually found ways to neutralize them. And these methods have been often been handed down as canon, unchallenged by modern players. Yet if one examines the top-level games of the past couple of years there is a remarkable renaissance of exactly these sorts of openings, such as the Four Knights Game, Closed Sicilian, and Slav.

These old-fashioned lines have the advantage that they have not been examined in the modern chess laboratories, and they still hold many undivulged secrets. At the same time, they can be learned quickly, because there is not the huge amount of collective wisdom (the ever-elusive "theory") sitting in every database.

This book includes a complete repertoire for Black. The openings do not require a great deal of memorization or deep understanding of positional nuances. They will allow the reader to emerge from the opening with a playable position. The variations are unlikely to lead to quick wins for Black, though some of the examples presented demonstrate that White can get crushed early in the game if he does not play carefully. On the other hand, if White plays with precision some of the lines presented here will not provide full equality. This should not come as a surprise, since there are no known defenses to the major openings which guarantee equality. When constructing a repertoire which does not require a tremendous amount of study, it is sometimes necessary to settle for second best. Nevertheless, the variations chosen for this book will never allow White more than a very slight advantage if Black plays with an understanding of the opening. Such advantages are easily eroded when White lacks the positional finesse of a World Champion, and therefore the recommended lines should be very effective in practical tournament play.

The Open Game (1.e4 e5)

Against 1.e4, 1...e5 has been the move most highly praised by chess teachers. Indeed, Gary Kasparov has said that if you have never played the Spanish Game (Ruy Lopez), you haven't really played chess, and I agree completely. There are a large number of variations in the Spanish Game, many of which require either a deep understanding of positional chess or a bloodlust which often leads to recklessness. The lines we will be examining, namely, the Classical variation (3...Bc5) is a solid and

straightforward opening which has retained its vitality, though it lacks
the popularity of the 3...a6 lines. It has the advantage of avoiding the
Exchange Variation (3...a6 4.Bxc6) which discourages some players
from adopting the Spanish, though it is considered relatively harmless at
the Grandmaster level. In addition, it is not encountered so frequently
in amateur play, rendering detailed knowledge of opening theory pretty
much moot.

The Spanish is not the only reaction to 1.e4. There are many "Open
Games" which must be taken into consideration. Most are fairly
harmless, though they often contain traps, and even the innocent
Scotch and Four Knights Games have been known to bushwack high-
level opponents, even if they are well-prepared. On the other hand,
there are good reasons why these lines are not frequently employed in
Grandmaster play. Much of the theory has been well worked out over
the past century, and it is difficult to find convincing innovations
against the recommended lines for Black. In our repertoire we will
adopt some of the standard remedies, but will also explore less well
traveled paths which can lead to equality without risk.

The most common alternative to the Spanish Game is the Italian
Game (1.e4 e5 2.Nf3 Nc6 3.Bc4). This is an established opening with a
vast body of theory, particularly in the lines after 3...Nf6 or 3...Bc5, so
we will adopt the Hungarian Defense with 3...d6. Although Black's
position is a little bit cramped, he has excellent fighting resources, as
Bent Larsen has demonstrated in similar lines of the Philidor Defense.

The Scotch Game has been revived by World Champion Gary
Kasparov, and its twin brother the Scotch Gambit has always been a
favorite among amateur players. Scotch Gambit players in particular
tend to be well-prepared, and I have some confidence in the White
side, having recently written a book advocating it. There are neutralizing
lines, but these tend to require a lot of knowledge of theory. I have
chosen a defense which is a bit cramped, but quite solid.

Other lines after 1.e4 e5 2.Nf3 Nc6 cause few problems for Black and
it is not difficult to obtain full equality. Some are a bit trappy, however,
so it pays to be familiar with them.

Alternatives at White's second move are especially popular in club
play. In the companion volume, I suggest 2.Bc4 as a good weapon for
White, and were it easy to equalize against it I would not have
recommended it. So I am in the awkward position of having to find a
good line against the very weapon I encourage the reader to use as
White! But with a little thought it becomes obvious that there must be at
least one opening in each player's repertoire which must be played
from both sides of the board. If the reader is adopting the entire
repertoire suggested in these two books, then the Bishop's opening is

where the overlap occurs. Again the preferred option is an unambitious but simple defense.

The King's Gambit is not to be feared, or so I argued in my book "Who's Afraid of the King's Gambit" (Chess Enterprises 1990). But while I have great confidence in the defenses presented there, the study of those lines is a major task which falls outside the goals of the practical repertoire. Here I choose a solid and straightforward plan which has stood the test of time. Most importantly, White's tiny advantage is positional in nature, and most King's Gambit afficionados at the amateur level are romantics who seek sacrificial glory. No bloodbath's in the Modern Defense, however, and thus a psychological advantage to the second player.

The Vienna Game is often employed to avoid the heavily travelled paths of "theory". There are many ways to equalize against it, but I have chosen one of the most obscure, which may well take the opponent out of his opening book.

Other flotsam and jetsam are more or less harmless, though one must be prepared for the gambit variations which can follow 2.d4

The Closed Game (1.d4 d5)

As in the case of the Open Game, we stay with classical themes and choose to meet the advance of White's d-pawn with a symmetrical reply. The Queen's Gambit is almost as rich as the Spanish Game in terms of the diverse approaches which can be employed by Black. Interestingly, it is another Exchange Variation (1.d4 d5 2.c4 e6 3.Nc3 Nf6 4.Bg5 Be7 5.cxd5 exd5) which often scares off the defenders at the amateur level, though here too it is considered relatively innocuous in Grandmaster play. We will avoid that variation by using the move order introduced by Alapin and refined by Alatortsev.

White does not have to offer a Queen's Gambit, of course, and in recent years the move 2.Nf3 has shown enormous popularity. White retains options of heading for a Torre Attack or Catalan or Yusupov-Zukertort or Colle, as well as more obscure plans. For this reason I think that it is important for Black to adopt a strategy which will determine the structural properties of the opening. 2...Bg4, attacking the Nf3, is an appropriate reply.

The Veresov (2.Nc3) is an ineffective opening which allows Black to play with a bit of aggression. The Blackmar-Diemer Gambit, on the other hand, is a reckless attempt to introduce attacking themes early in the game. Black should play solidly, and should keep in mind that BDG players tend to know the theory of their pet line very well indeed.

Other moves pose even less danger in the Closed Game than in the Open Game.

Flank Openings

The English Opening is largely irrelevant to our discussion. After 1.c4 e6 Black will play 2...d5, and then White will either have to transpose to the Queen's Gambit or adopt a Reti formation. The Catalan represents a compromise between the two strategies. In each case Black will set up a very solid formation with pawns at c6, d5 and e6 and develop his pieces normally.

The Bird Opening (1.f4) will be met aggresively by 1...e5, the From Gambit. If White accepts, we will adopt the newly popular approach with 2...Nc6. If there is a transposition to the King's Gambit with 2.e4, that is fine with us, too. The discussion of the From is derived from my 1992 monograph on that opening.

The Nimzowitsch Attack (1.Nf3, intending 2.b3) and the immediate 1.b3 are met by similar strategies, involving the establishment of a strong pawn at e5.

Unorthodoxy

Almost every legal move is seen in the opening, especially in informal play. While there is no room in this book to present an exhaustive analysis or even compilation of the oddities one may encounter early in the game, I have chosen a number of examples which illustrate effective strategies for Black. Those who are obsessed with such diversions and perversions are referred to Unorthodox Openings (Benjamin & Schiller, 1987), but I trust the reader will find sufficient material in this volume to inspire the necessary confidence.

The Classical Spanish Game
(1.e4 e5 2.Nf3 Nc6 3.Bb5 Bc5)

This is one of the oldest lines of the Spanish Game, and usually leads to exciting play with chances for both sides to score the full point. There are two move orders which are used by Black. The first involves 3...Nf6 4.0-0 Bc5 and the other is 3...Bc5. The only difference is in the options available to White on his fourth move, and 3...Nf6 is generally considered the safest path.

White plays 5.Nxe5
Krogius–Spassky
USSR Championship, 1959
1.e4 e5 2.Nf3 Nc6 3.Bb5 Nf6 4.0-0 Bc5 5.Nxe5

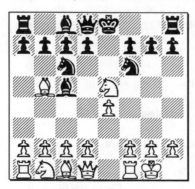

This is a very direct move by White, but it leads to complications which are not unfavorable for the second player.

| 5... | Nxe5 |
| 6.d4 | c6!? |

This move accomplishes two things. It challenges the Bb5 and also provides important support for the critical d5 square.

7.dxe5

7.Ba4 Nxe4 8.Re1 d5 is good for Black, for example: 9.dxc5 0-0 10.Qd4 Qf6! (threatening Nf3+) 11.Be3 Bh3! (renewing the threat) 12.Kh1 Bxg2+ 13.Kxg2 Qf3+! 14.Kg1 Qg4+ 15.Kh1 Nf3 16.Qd1 Qh3 and Black resigned in Hofmann–Lambert, Vienna 1947.

7...	Nxe4
8.Bd3	

8.Qg4 has a bark that is worse than its bite. 8...Nxf2! 9.Qxg7 Ne4+ 10.Kh1 Rf8 and Black should have little difficulty consolidating, after which an attack on the kingside is a distinct possibility.

8...	d5
9.exd6	

9.Qf3 Qh4 10.g3 Bg4! 11.Qf4 g5 and the complications favored Black in DeGroot–O'Kelly, Beverwijk 1946.

9...	Nf6!
10.Qe2+	

10.Bg5 see the next game.

10.Bf4 Bxd6 11.Bxd6 Qxd6 12.Nc3 Be6 13.Qe2 0-0 =. Aronin–Keres, USSR Championship 1952.

10...	Be6
11.Bg5	Qxd6!
12.Bxf6	

12.Nc3 Ng4 13.g3 Bd4!? (13...Ne5 14.Bf4 f6 15.Ne4 Qe7 16.Nxc5 Qxc5 17.Bxe5 fxe5 18.Rfe1 ±) 14.Ne4 Qc7 15.c3 Bb6 is complex, but perhaps the weakening of the light squares on the kingside gives Black enough play.

12...	gxf6
13.Nd2	Qe5!

Clearly an exchange of queens will lead to a favorable position for Black, who owns the bishop pair.

14.Ne4	Bb6
15.Kh1	

The point of this move is to unpin the f-pawn.

15...	0-0-0!
16.a4	Kb8

Black has a good position and is in no hurry here.

17.a5	Bc7
18.f4	Qd4
19.Nc3	

19.Ng3 Bxf4 20.Nh5 Be5 ∓

19...	f5

19...Bxf4? 20.a6! with counterplay.

20.a6

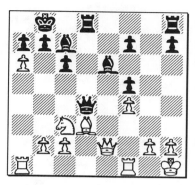

20...	b5!
21.Qf3	Qb6!

Now Black has secured his defenses.

22.Qh3	Qc5
23.Qf3	b4
24.Na4	Qd6!

Black's forces remain coordinated while White's seem to be scattered all over the board.

25.Qh3	Rhg8
26.Be2	

26.Bxf5 is met strongly by 26...Bd5.

26...	Qd2
27.Bf3	Bc4
28.Rfd1	Qxf4

The game is effectively over at this point.

29.Rxd8+ Rxd8 30.Bxc6 Be2 31.Rg1 Rd1 32.g4 Rxg1+ 33.Kxg1 Qc1+ 34.Kf2 Qxc2 35.Qxh7 Bb5+ 36.Kg1 Qd1+ 37.Kf2 Qf1+ 38.Ke3 Qf4# 0-1.

Sigurjonsson–Taulbut
Brighton, 1981

1.e4 e5 2.Nf3 Nc6 3.Bb5 Nf6 4.0-0 Bc5 5.Nxe5 Nxe5 6.d4 c6 7.dxe5 Nxe4 8.Bd3 d5 9.exd6 Nf6 10.Bg5

The main line. For alternatives, see Krogius–Spassky, above.

| 10... | Bxd6 |
| 11.Re1+ | |

An obvious move. The only known alternative was recently introduced into play.

11.Nc3 Be6 12.Re1 transposes to the game.

11...	Be6
12.Nc3	Qc7!
13.Bxf6	gxf6

White has created a weakness on the kingside, but it only opens up lines that lead directly to his king, and the bishop pair will be an effective fighting force.

| 14.Qh5 | 0-0-0 |
| 15.Ne4 | Bb4 |

15...Be5 is also very strong, Renet–Winants, Lyon Zonal 1990.

16.Re2

16.c3 Rxd3 17.cxb4 Rg8 18.Qxh7 Rdd8! gives Black two open files on the kingside.

| 16... | Qf4! |
| 17.g3 | Rhg8 |

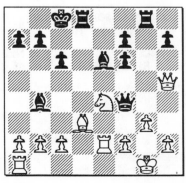

18.Re3	f5
19.Nf6	Rg5

White's pieces are hopelessly tangled. 20.Qe2 Bc5 21.Nh5 Qd6 22.h4 Rxh5 White resigned here, because after the rooks come off the White pawns fall like rotten apples. 0-1.

White plays 5.c3

Schlosser–Anand
Prestwich, 1990

1.e4 e5 2.Nf3 Nc6 3.Bb5 Nf6 4.0-0 Bc5 5.c3 0-0 6.d4 Bb6 7.Re1

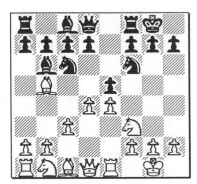

This is a solid a cautious move, but Black already has enough of a presence in the center to begin active play.

7...	exd4!
8.e5	

8.cxd4 is discussed in Letriguilly–Dezan.

8...	Ng4!
9.Bg5!?	

9.h3 Nxf2 10.Kxf2 f6 creates a lot of threats. Although the position requires practical tests I think that Black has more than enough compensation.

9.cxd4? Nxd4 10.Nxd4 Qh4-+

9...	Nxf2
10.Qa4	

10.Kxf2 Qxg5 (10...f6!?) 11.Nxg5 dxc3+ 12Kf1 cxb2 13.Qc2+-

10...	dxc3
11.Bxd8	cxb2
12.Bxc7	

One of the strangest positions I have ever seen.

12...	bxa1Q
13.Bxb6	axb6
14.Qxa8	

Again, the bizarre tableau deserves a picture. Black is two pawns ahead, if you are having problems keeping count. But his bishop at c8 is pretty sad.

14...	Qb2
15.Qa4	Ng4!
16.Qxg4	Qxb5
17.Qg3	Qc5+
18.Kh1	f6
19.exf6	Rxf6
20.Nbd2	d5

Now things have settled down, and Black is in command.

21.Ng5	Rf8
22.Ndf3	h6
23.Nh3	Qb4
24.Nhg1	Bf5

25.Qc7	Be4
26.Rd1	Qe7!
27.Qxb6	Ne5
28.Qe3	Ng4
29.Qd4	Qa3
30.h3	Ne3
31.Rd2	Nf1
32.Rf2	Ng3+
33.Kh2	Qd6!
34.Ne5	Nf5

34...Rxf2 35.Qxf2 Qxe5 36.Qxg3 Qxg3+ 37.Kxg3 Kf7 38.Ne2 Kf6 should also win, but it would be more time-consuming.

35.Qb2 Re8 36.Rxf5 Bxf5 37.Ngf3 Be4-+ 38.Kg1 Qf6 39.Qxb7 Kh7 40.Qc7 Re7 41.Qb8 Qf4 42.Qb2 h5

There is nothing White can do about the advance of the kingside pawns. 0-1.

Letreguilly–Dezan
France, 1989

1.e4 e5 2.Nf3 Nc6 3.Bb5 Nf6 4.0-0 Bc5 5.c3 0-0 6.d4 Bb6 7.Re1 exd4 8.cxd4 d5 9.e5 Ne4 10.Nc3 Bg4 11.Bxc6 bxc6 12.Nxe4 dxe4 13.Rxe4 Bxf3 14.Qxf3 Bxd4 15.Bh6?

15.Be3 Bxb2 16.Rb1 f5! 17.exf6 was agreed drawn in Unzicker–Fischer, Leipzig Olympiad 1960.

15...	f5
16.Qg3	

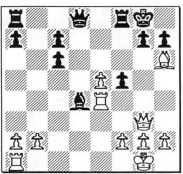

16...Bxf2+! 17.Qxf2 fxe4 18.Qg3 Qe7 ∓ 19.Rc1 Rad8 20.h3 Rd3 21.Qe1 Qxe5 22.Be3 Qxb2 23.Rxc6 Rfd8 24.Rc1 Qxc1!! 25.Qxc1 Rd1+ 0-1.

Hardicsay–Knezevic
Budapest, 1976

**1.e4 e5 2.Nf3 Nc6 3.Bb5 Nf6 4.0-0 Bc5 5.c3 0-0 6.d4 Bb6
7.Bg5 h6 8.Bh4**

8.Bxc6 hxg5 9.Ba4 Nxe4 10.Nxe5 d5 11.Nd2 Nd6 12.Qh5 Qf6 13.f4
gxf4 14.Bc2 g6 15.Qh6 Qxe5 0-1., Houston–Lane, British Championship,
1989

**8...   d6
9.a4**

This is perhaps the most common move, since it virtually forces
Black's reply and creates a weakness on Black's queenside. There are,
however, alternatives.

a) 9.Qd3 Qe7 10.Nbd2 Bd7 and now 11.Rfe1 (11.a4 a6 12.dxe5 Nxe5
13.Nxe5 dxe5 14.Bxf6 Bxb5 15.axb5 Qxf6 16.bxa6 Rxa6 17.Rxa6 bxa6
18.Nc4 Rd8 19.Qe2 Qe6 20.h3 f6 21.Ra1 Ba7 22.h4 h5 23.Na5 Qb6 24.g3
g6 25.Kg2 Kg7 26.Ra2 Rd7 27.Nc4 Qc6 28.Ra5 Rd8 29.b3 Kh7 30.Ra4
Qb7 31.Rb4 Qc6 32.Qf3 Bb6 33.Ra4 Ba7 34.Ra2 Kg7 35.Ra5 Qb7 36.Ra4
Qxb3 37.Rxa6 Rf8 38.Na5 Qb8 39.Re6 Rf7 40.Qd3 Qb2 41.Qf1 Qc2
42.Ra6 Bc5 43.Nc6 Rd7 44.Nb4 Qxe4+ 45.Kh2 Rd2 46.Ra2 Rxa2 47.Nxa2
Qf3 48.Qg2 Qxf2 0-1., Dorfman–Gulko, Moscow, 1978) 11...a6?! (Better
is 11...Na5, after which Black has a fine game.) 12.Bc4 Bg4 13.Bb3 Ba7
14.Ba4 b5 15.Bc2 Rfe8 16.h3 Bh5 17.Bg3 a5 18.Nh4 exd4 19.Nf5 Qd7
20.Bh4 Bg6 21.Bxf6 gxf6 22.Nxd4 Bxd4 23.cxd4 Nb4 24.Qb3 c5 25.Bb1
Nc6 26.Nf3 Kg7 27.d5 Ne5 28.Nh4 c4 29.Qg3 Qa7 30.Kh2 Kh7 31.f4 Nd7
32.Qg4 Rg8 33.Re2 Kh8 34.Qf3 Qd4 35.Qe3 Qd1 36.Re1 Qh5 37.Qf2 1-0,
Kuporosov–Tatar Kis, Budapest Spring Open, 1990.

b) 9.Re1 Bg4 10.Bxc6 bxc6 11.dxe5 dxe5 can be played without the
inclusion of the advance of the a-pawns, e.g., King–Knezevic,
Wuppertal, 1986: 12.Qxd8 Raxd8 13.Nxe5 g5 14.Bg3 Nxe4! 15.Nxg4 f5
16.Na3 Nxg3 17.Nxh6+ 1/2–1/2.

c) 9.d5 Nb8 10.Nbd2 c6 11.Bd3 Nbd7 12.c4 a5 13.Re1 Re8 14.Rc1 Nf8
15.Bb1 Ng6 16.Bg3 Rf8 17.dxc6 bxc6 18.c5 Bxc5 19.Nb3 Bb4 20.Nfd2
Be6 21.Rxc6 a4 22.Nc1 Bc5 23.Qe2 Qa5 24.Nd3 Bd7 25.Rxc5 dxc5
26.Nc4 Qa6 27.Nxc5 Qc6 28.Nxd7 Nxd7 29.Ne3 Nb6 30.Nd5 Rfd8
31.Bxe5 Nxd5 32.exd5 Qxd5 33.Bxg6 fxg6 34.a3 Re8 35.f4 g5 36.Qg4
Rad8 37.h4 Qd7 38.f5 gxh4 39.Kh2 Re7 40.Qxh4 Rde8 41.Qc4+ Kh8
42.Qf4 Qd5 43.f6 Rxe5 44.f7 Rxe1 0-1, Jonsson-A.Martin, Hringey 1988.

**9...   a5
10.d5**

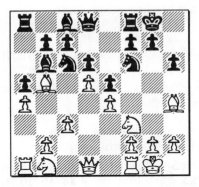

Not a good idea at all. It only opens up the diagonal for the bishop at b6.

Ciric–Van Geet, Beverwijk, 1967 proceeded more quietly, but things turned out well for Black in the end: 10.Re1 Bg4 11.Bxc6 bxc6 12.dxe5 dxe5 13.Qxd8 Raxd8 14.Nxe5 g5 15.Bg3 Nxe4 16.Nxg4 f5 17.Bxc7 Bxc7 18.Na3 fxg4 19.Rxe4 Rd2 20.Nc4 Rdxf2 21.Rae1 g3 22.hxg3 Bxg3 23.R4e3 Bb8 24.Rf3 Ba7 25.Rxf8+ Kxf8 26.Kh2 Bb8+ 27.Kh1 Bg3 28.Rd1 Rf5 29.Kg1 g4 30.b4 axb4 31.cxb4 Rf4 32.Na5 Rxb4 33.Nxc6 Rxa4 34.Nd4 Bb8 35.Rf1+ Kg7 36.Nf5+ Kg6 37.g3 Kg5 38.Kh1 Ra5 39.Rb1 Be5 40.Rf1 Ra3 41.Kg2 Ra2+ 42.Kh1 Rb2 43.Kg1 Bb8 44.Kh1 h5 45.Kg1 Rb5 46.Ng7 Bxg3 47.Ne6+ Kg6 48.Nf8+ Kh6 49.Ne6 Be5 50.Nd8 Kg6 51.Kh1 Rb6 52.Re1 Kf5 53.Rc1 Rb2 54.Nc6 Bf4 55.Ne7+ Ke4 56.Re1+ Kf3 57.Nd5 Bg3 58.Rc1 0-1.

Sibarevic–Knezevic, Yugoslavia, 1976, on the other hand, was an absolute disaster for White: 10.Bxc6 bxc6 11.dxe5 dxe5 12.Qxd8 Rxd8 13.Re1 Ba6 14.Nbd2 g5 0-1.

10...	Nb8
11.Nbd2	c6
12.Bc4	Nbd7
13.h3	cxd5
14.exd5	Qc7
15.Qe2	Nh5
16.Kh2	Nf4
17.Qd1	f5
18.Ng1	

White's position demonstrates the poverty of his strategy. Neither bishop is being at all helpful and the rest of the forces lie back on the first two ranks.

18...	Ng6
19.Qh5	Kh7
20.Ne2	e4

Now the queen has lost her escape route.

   21.Bb5   **Nxh4**

   22.Bxd7

22.Qxh4 g5 23.Qh5 (23.Qg3 f4 24.Qg4 Nf6) 23...Nf6 traps the lady.

   22...   **Bxd7**

Black resigned, because of 23.Qxh4 g5 24.Qg3 f4 25.Nxf4 gxf4 26.Qh4 Rae8.

Nijboer–Anand
Wijk aan Zee, 1990

1.e4 e5 2.Nf3 Nc6 3.Bb5 Nf6 4.0-0 Bc5 5.c3 0-0 6.d4 Bb6 7.Bg5 h6 8.Bh4 d6 9.a4 a5 10.Bxc6

10.Qd3 Qe7 11.Nbd2 Rd8 12.Rfe1 Bg4 13.Nc4 Bxf3 14.Qxf3 exd4 15.Bxc6 bxc6 16.e5 Re8! 17.Bxf6 gxf6 18.cxd4 Qe6 19.Nxb6 cxb6 20.Ra3 fxe5 21.Rae3 Rac8 22.dxe5 dxe5 23.Qh5 Rcd8 and a draw was agreed in Chandler–Braga, Ostend 1984.

10...bxc6 11.Nbd2 Ba6 12.Re1 Qe7 13.d5 g5 14.Nxg5 hxg5 15.Bxg5 Kg7 16.b4 cxd5 17.exd5 Qd7 18.Qf3 Nh7 19.Qh5 f5 20.b5 Bb7 21.Bh6+ Kh8 22.Bxf8 Rxf8 23.Nc4 f4 24.Rad1 Bc8 25.Nxb6 cxb6 26.f3 Qc7 27.Qh4 Bf5 28.c4 Kg7 29.Rc1 Nf6 30.Qf2 Nd7 31.g3 Bg6 32.gxf4 Rxf4 33.Kh1 Nc5 34.Rg1 Qf7 35.Rcf1 Kf8 36.Rg3 Ne4 37.Qxb6 Nxg3+ 38.hxg3 Rf6 39.Qe3 e4 40.b6 exf3 41.Kg1 Bh5 42.Qd4 Kg7 43.Qb2 Kh7 44.Kf2 Qe7 45.g4 Rh6 46.b7 Qh4+ 47.Ke3 Qg5+ 48.Kd3 Bg6+ 0-1.

Wolff–Schiller
Pan American Intercollegiate, 1988

1.e4 e5 2.Nf3 Nc6 3.Bb5 Nf6 4.0-0 Bc5 5.c3 0-0 6.d4 Bb6 7.Bg5 h6 8.Bh4 d6 9.Bxc6 bxc6 10.dxe5 dxe5 11.Qa4

11.Nḃd2 is the main alternative, for example: 11...Re8 12.Qa4 g5 13.Bg3 g4 14.Rad1 gxf3 15.Nxf3 Qe7 16.Nxe5 Nh5 17.Qxc6 Nxg3 18.hxg3 Bb7 19.Qxb7 Qxe5 20.Qc6 Kg7 21.Rd3 Qxe4 22.Qxe4 Rxe4 0-1., Hellers–Finegold, Reykjavik, 1990, while Hellers managed to maintain a roughly level game by retreating the bishop: (after 11.Nbd2 Re8) 12.Bg3 (12.Qa4 g5 13.Bg3 g4!) 12...Nd7 13.b4 Qe7 14.Nc4 f6 15.Nfd2 Qe6 with compensation, Hellers–Van der Wiel, Haninge, 1990.

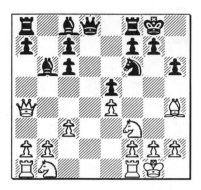

This move has the dual purpose of attacking the pawn at c6 and freeing the d-file for the rook.

11... **Qe8!?**

My novelty. The idea is that the fracturing of the pawn structure if White takes the knight is not terribly important. The bishop pair will then be very effective.

The alternatives include:

a) 11...Qd6 12.Na3 Nd7 13.Nc4 Qe6 14.Nxb6 cxb6 15.Rfd1 Nc5 16.Qc2 a5 17.b4 Nb7 18.Nd2 c5 19.a3 Bd7 20.f3 Rfc8 21.Qb2 Ba4 22.Rdc1 Rc7 23.Nf1 Nd6 24.Ne3 Nc4 25.Qf2 Nxe3 26.Qxe3 Bb3 27.Rab1 a4 28.Rb2 Rac8 29.bxc5 Rxc5 30.Rd2 f6 31.Bf2 R5c6 32.Rd3 Bc4 33.Rdd1 b5 34.Be1 Rd6 35.Rxd6 Qxd6 36.Ra1 Rd8 37.h3 Qc7 38.Bf2 Rd3 39.Qc5 Qd7 40.Rc1 Rd2 41.Qa7 Qe8 42.Qc5 Kh7 43.Be3 Rd3 44.Kh2 Qh5 45.Qb6 f5 46.exf5 Qxf5 47.Qc5 Rd5 48.Qe7 Qd3 49.Re1 Qf5 50.Bc1 Bd3 51.Kg1 Bc2 52.Kh2 Qf6 53.Qc7 Bd3 54.Re3 Qf4+ 55.g3 Qf5 56.g4 Qf4+ 57.Kg2 Bc4 58.Rd3 Qxc1 59.Rxd5 Qf1+ 60.Kg3 Qe1+ 0-1., Rachels–Torre, Manila Interzonal, 1990; and

b) 11...Qd3 12.Bxf6 gxf6 13.Qxc6 Be6 14.Nbd2 Rad8 15.h3 Kh7 16.a4 Rg8 17.Kh2 Be3 18.fxe3 Qe2 19.Rg1 Rxd2 20.Ne1 Qxe3 21.Kh1 Rg3 0-1., Hosticka–Krcmar, Karvina Open, 1989.

12.Bg3

12.Bxf6 gxf6 13.Nbd2 Bg4 14.h3 Bh5 15.Rad1 Rd8 =.

12... **c5!**

A paradoxical move, since it seems to turn the dark-squared bishop into a pawn. But the light-squares are available to the other bishop.

13.Qxe8	**Rxe8**
14.Re1	**Bb7**

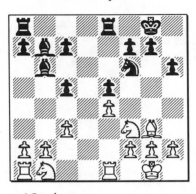

15.a4

15.Nbd2 Rad8 =.

15...	a5
16.Nbd2	Rad8
17.Rad1?	

A simple oversight. The rook at e1 is overworked.

17...	Nxe4!
18.Nxe4	Rxd1
19.Rxd1	Bxe4
20.Nxe5	Bc2

This is probably what Wolff missed in his calculations.

21.Rd2	Bxa4
22.h4	

Black has only a small advantage here, because the bishop at b6 serves no useful function.

22...	f6
23.Nc4	Bb3
24.Ne3	

24.Nxb6 cxb6 25.Bc7 Re6 26.Rd8+ Kf7 27.Rb8 Re1+ 28.Kh2 Re2 29.Bxb6 Rxb2 30.Bxc5 a4 31.Ra8 =.

24...	a4
25.c4	Re4
26.Rd8+	Kf7
27.Rd7+	

I should have played on, as the position is better for Black, but with the pressure of team competition and a lack of confidence, I accepted the offer of a draw. 1/2–1/2.

Klings–Gruen
Schoneck, 1988

1.e4 e5 2.Nf3 Nc6 3.Bb5 Nf6 4.0-0 Bc5 5.c3 0-0 6.d4 Bb6

7.dxe5

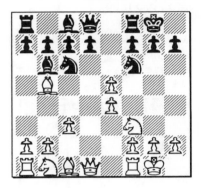

This is one of the most common replies.

7...	Nxe4
8.Qd5	Nc5
9.Bg5	

Mateo–Winants, Thessaloniki Olympiad, 1988 saw instead 9.b4 Ne7 10.Qd1 Ne4 11.a4 a6 12.Bd3 d5 13.exd6 Nxd6 14.c4 c5 15.Be3 Ndf5 16.Bxc5 Bxc5 17.bxc5 Qa5 18.Nbd2 Qxc5 19.Qb3 Nc6 20.Be4 Nd6 21.Bd5 Bf5 22.Qa3 Qxa3 23.Rxa3 Nb4 24.Rb3 Nxd5 25.cxd5 b5 26.axb5 axb5 27.Nd4 Bd7 28.N2f3 Ra4 29.h3 Rc8 30.Rd1 Rcc4 31.Nc6 f6 32.Nfd4 Bxc6 33.Nxc6 Re4 34.Rb2 h5 35.f3 Re8 36.Nd4 Rb8 37.Rc2 Nc4 38.Nc6 Rba8 39.Re2 Ra1 40.Rxa1 Rxa1+ 41.Kf2 Rd1 42.Re8+ Kf7 43.Rd8 Rd2+ 44.Ke1 Rxg2 45.Nd4 Ke7 46.Nc6+ Kf7 47.Nd4 Ke7 48.Nc6+ 1/2–1/2.

9...   **Qe8**

The last few moves were virtually forced, though Black could have interposed at his last turn. The text is more ambitious.

10.Na3

a) 10.Nbd2 is inferior after 10...d6! with the idea of Be6 . e.g.,

a1) 11.Nd4 Qxe5 12.Bxc6 bxc6 13.Qxe5 (13.Qxc6 Bb7-+) dxe5 14.N4f3 Nd3! ∓;

a2) 11.exd6 Be6 12.Bxc6 (12.d7 Qb8! 13.d8Q Nxd8 14.Bxd8 Rxd8 15.Qg5 c6 ∓) bxc6 13.Qd4? f6! 14.Rae1 (14.Be3 Nb3) Qg6 15.Bh4 Bd5 16.Re2 Ne4 17.Qd3 Ng3! 18.Qa6 (18.Qxg6 Nxe2+ 19.Kh1 hxg6) Nxf1! 19.Kxf1 cxd6 20.Bg3 Rfe8 21.Bxd6 Rxe2 22.Qxe2 Re8 Gipslis–Spassky, Riga 1959.

b) 10.Re1 Qe6 11.Qxe6 Nxe6 =. Matanovic–Ivkov, Leberg 1962.

c) 10.b4 Ne6 11.Bh4 Ne7 is better for Black.

10...	Ne6!
11.Bh4	

11.Nc4 Nxg5 12.Nxg5 Ne7 13.Qe4 Ng6 14.h4 c6 15.Nxb6 axb6 16.Bd3 d5 17.exd6 Qxe4 18.Bxe4 Nxh4 19.Bxh7+ Kh8 20.Bd3 f6 21.Ne4 Be6 22.a3 Rad8 23.Rad1 Nf5 24.Bc2 Bd5 =

| 11... | Ne7! |

Prasad–Anand, New Delhi 1990 varied with 11...a6.

12.Qe4	Ng6
13.Rae1	a6
14.Bc4	

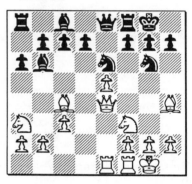

| 14... | Rb8 |
| 15.Nc2 | Ba7! |

Black is now ready to expand on the queenside.

| 16.b4 | b5 |
| 17.Bb3 | Bb7 |

Black's pieces are clearly more active.

18.Bd5	c6
19.Bb3	Nef4
20.Ne3	c5!
21.Qf5	c4
22.Bd1	Bxe3
23.Rxe3	

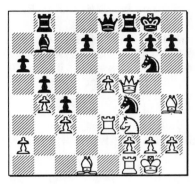

| 23... | Nxg2! |
| 24.Bg3 | |

24.Kxg2 Nxh4+

24...	Nxe3
25.fxe3	Qe6
26.Qh5	Qd5
27.Bc2	Rbe8

White has no compensation at all for his material.

28.Bf5 h6 29.e4 Qd3 30.Qg4 Qxc3 31.Bxd7 Qe3+ 32.Rf2 Bxe4 33.Bxe8 Rxe8 34.Qd7 Rf8 35.Kg2 Nxe5! 36.Bxe5 Bxf3+ 0-1.

Jackson,S–Garcia,N
Dubai Olympiad, 1986

1.e4 e5 2.Nf3 Nc6 3.Bb5 Nf6 4.0-0 Bc5 5.c3 0-0 6.d4 Bb6

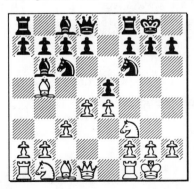

The minor variations discussed in this game are not without merit, and Black should be prepared to meet them.

7.d5

7.Nxe5 Nxe5 8.dxe5 Nxe4 9.Nd2 Nxd2 10.Bxd2 f6 = W.Schmidt–Rellstab, Hamburg 1955.

7.Bxc6 bxc6 8.Nxe5 Nxe4 9.Re1 Nd6 10.Bf4 a5 11.c4 f6 12.c5 fxe5 13.Bxe5 Nc4 14.cxb6 Nxb6 15.Nc3 d6 16.Bg3 Qf6 17.Rc1 Bd7 18.Qb3+ Qf7 19.Qxf7+ Kxf7 and a draw was agreed in O'Kelly–Karaklaic, Bognor Regis 1960. But I think that Black stands better here, so Black need not worry much about this line.

7...   Ne7
8.Nxe5

8.Bd3 d6 9.Na3 c6 10.c4 Bg4 11.h3 Bh5 12.Bg5 Nd7 13.g4 f6! 14.Bd2 Nc5 15.Bc2 Bg6 was roughly even in Bannik–Klaman, USSR Championship 1957.

8...   d6
9.Nc4   Nxe4
10.Nxb6   axb6
11.Be2   Nf6

White has the bishop pair, but also the burden of defending the pawn at d5.

12.c4   b5!
13.b3   bxc4
14.bxc4   Ng6
15.Nc3   Ne5
16.h3   Re8
17.Be3

17.Bg5!?

17...   Nfd7
18.Bd4   Nc5

Knights like these are always worth a pair of bishops!

19.f4 Ned7 20.Qd2 Nb6 21.f5 f6 22.Rae1 Nbd7 23.Rf4 b6 24.Bh5 Rxe1+ 25.Qxe1 Ne5 26.Qe3 Qe7 27.Kh2 Bd7 1/2–1/2.

Hobbis–Cooper
Correspondence, 1952

**1.e4 e5 2.Nf3 Nc6 3.Bb5 Nf6 4.0-0 Bc5 5.c3 0-0 6.Re1?! d5!
7.Bxc6 bxc6 8.Nxe5 dxe4**

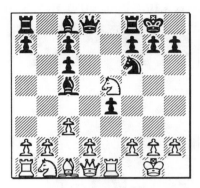

Black already has a good game, despite the fractured pawn structure Now White grabs a pawn and digs his own grave.

9.Nxc6?	Qd6
10.d4	

10.Nd4 Bxd4 11.cxd4 Qxd4 ∓ with the idea of Ba6.

10...	Ng4
11.dxc5??	

11.g3 Qxc6 12.dxc5 Qxc5 13.Qd4 Qh5 14.h4 Bb7 with a very strong attack.

11...	Qxh2+
12.Kf1	Ba6+

Compare this position with the end of Amateur–Sewell to see the same theme at work 0-1.

White captures on c6

Van der Wiel–Salov
Rotterdam, 1989

1.e4 e5 2.Nf3 Nc6 3.Bb5 Nf6 4.0-0 Bc5 5.Bxc6 dxc6 6.d3

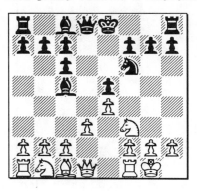

6.Nxe5 Nxe4 7.Qe2 Qd5 8.d4 Bxd4 9.Nf3 Be6 10.c4 Qxc4 11.Qxc4 Bxf2+ 12.Rxf2 Bxc4 13.Nc3 Nxf2 14.Kxf2 0-0-0 ∓, Zapata–Rohde, New York Open, 1988.

This wimpy move does nothing to justify the loss of the bishop pair.

6...	Qe7
7.Nbd2	Bg4
8.Nc4	Nd7

Black has developed smoothly and has plenty of support for e5. His position is at least as good as White's, if not better.

9.Be3	Bd6!

9...Bxe3 10.fxe3 would allow White to swing his queen to g3 via e1, and get a good game with pressure on the f-file.

10.h3

10.Nxd6+ cxd6 is perhaps a touch better for Black, who has more plans, e.g., d6–d5 or f7–f5.

10...	Bh5
11.a4	f6
12.c3	b6

12...b5? 13.axb5 cxb5 14.Nxd6+ cxd6 15.Rxa7

13.Re1	0-0
14.Bc1	

White wants to use e3 for the knight.

14...	Rfd8
15.Ne3	Qf7
16.Nf5	Bf8

Black threatens Nc5.

17.Be3	Nc5
18.Bxc5	Bxc5

Black now has a clear advantage, thanks to the bishop pair and the weakness of the pawn at d3.

19.a5	b5
20.Ng3	Bg6
21.Qc2	Qe6
22.b4	Bf8

White has succeeded in driving back the bishop, but the pawn structure on the queenside is vulnerable.

23.d4	exd4
24.Nxd4	Qc4!
25.Qa2	

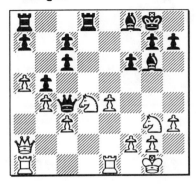

White hopes that the exchange of queens will bring about an ending where the kingside pawn majority and weakness at c6 will give him some chances. But...

25...	Bxb4!
26.Nxb5	

26.Qxc4+ bxc4 27.cxb4 Rxd4 ∓

26...	Qxa2
27.Rxa2	Bf7!
28.Raa1	Bxa5
29.Rxa5	cxb5
30.Rea1	

30.Rxb5 Rd3 31.Rc5 a5 32.Rxc7 a4 33.Ra1 a3 and the rook cannot get back from c7 in time.

30...	Rdb8
31.Nf5	

31.Rxa7 Rxa7 32.Rxa7 Rc8 33.Rb7 Bc4 ∓

31...	Rb7

Black's position is passive, but the queenside pawns are more than worth the price.

32.Nd4	Bc4
33.Nc6	

White can now regain the pawn. but the endgame is still clearly better for Black.

33...Kf7 34.Nxa7 c5 35.f3 Bd3 36.Kf2 b4 37.Nc6 Rxa5 38.Nxa5 Rc7 39.Ke3 Bc2 40.Kd2 b3 41.Nc4 Rd7+ 42.Kc1 Rd1+ 43.Kb2 Rxa1 44.Kxa1

44...	Bd3
45.Nd2	c4
46.g3	g5
47.f4	gxf4
48.gxf4	Kg6

It is the relative mobility of the kings that gives Black the game.

49.Kb2	Kh5
50.Kc1	Kh4
51.Kb2	h5
52.Ka3	Kxh3
53.e5	fxe5
54.fxe5	Bf5
55.Nxc4	h4
56.Ne3	

56.Kxb3 Kg3 57.Ne3 Be6+-+

56...Be6 57.c4 Kg3 58.Kxb3 h3 59.Kc3 Kf2 0-1.

Other 5th moves for White

Amateur–Sewell
Correspondence, 1951

1.e4 e5 2.Nf3 Nc6 3.Bb5 Nf6 4.0-0 Bc5 5.Re1 Ng4

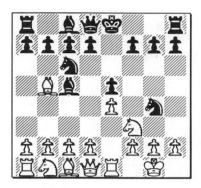

6.d4?

6.Re2 Nd4 7.Nxd4 Bxd4 8.h3 Nxf2 9.Rxf2 Qh4 10.Qe2 Bxf2+ 11.Qxf2 Qxe4 12.d3 Qd4 13.Qxd4 exd4 14.Bc4 c6 ∓

6...	exd4
7.Nxd4	Qh4
8.Bxc6	bxc6
9.Be3	Qxh2+
10.Kf1	Ba6+
11.Re2	Qh1+# 0-1

Black plays 3...Nf6 and White doesn't castle
Mayet–Anderssen
Berlin, 1862

1.e4 e5 2.Nf3 Nc6 3.Bb5 Nf6 4.d3 Bc5 5.c3 0-0 6.0-0 d5

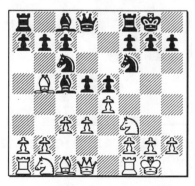

When White plays passively Black can quickly seize the initiative.

7.Bxc6	bxc6
8.Nxe5	dxe4

8...Qd6!? 9.d4 Nxe4

9.d4	**Bb6**
10.f4?	

White believes that the a7–g1 diagonal holds no danger for him. Wrong.

10...	**c5!**
11.dxc5	**Bxc5+**
12.Kh1	**Bb7**

Black has two very powerful clerics aimed at the White king, whose chances of survival are not great.

13.c4

An attempt to control d5 and give space to the knight at b1.

13...	**Re8**
14.a3	

14.Nc3 was more logical.

14...	**e3!**
15.Qe2	**Qd4**
16.Nc3	**Rad8**
17.Nb5	**Qe4**
18.b4	

18.Rg1 Rxe5! 19.fxe5 Ng4

18.Nc3! Qf5 19.Bxe3 Bxe3 20.Qxe3 Ng4 21.Qg3 Nxe5 22.fxe5 Qxe5 ∓

18...	**Nh5!**

19.bxc5 Nxf4 20.Rxf4 Rd1+!! 21.Rf1 Qxg2+ 22.Qxg2 Rxf1#
A beautiful finish! 0-1.

Neumann–Anderssen
Berlin, 1864

1.e4 e5 2.Nf3 Nc6 3.Bb5 Nf6 4.d3 Bc5 5.c3 0-0 6.Bxc6

This is just a waste of time. White should return to normal lines by castling.

6...   **bxc6**

Usually Black will recapture with the d-pawn in these positions, but here the initiative Black gets is well worth the investment of the e-pawn.

7.Nxe5

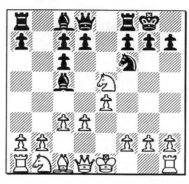

7...   **d5!**

Black offers yet another pawn in the opening!

8.0-0   **dxe4**

9.d4

9.dxe4 Qxd1 10.Rxd1 Nxe4 11.Be3 Bxe3 12.fxe3 Re8! 13.Nxc6 Bb7 14.Nd4 Rad8 15.Na3 (15.Nd2 Nxd2 16.Rxd2 Rxe3 ∓) Nc5 16.Kf2 Rd6 and Black has plenty of compensation for the pawn.

9...   **Bd6**

10.Nxc6   **Qe8**

This is a typical sacrificial plan in the Classical Spanish. Black gives up a doubled and useless c-pawn while transferring his queen to a useful post at e8. The dynamic potential of the Black forces is quite high, as the White king is weak.

11.Na5

11.Ne5 Bxe5 12.dxe5 Qxe5 is clearly better for Black, but exiling the knight to the edge of the board was hardly an improvement, even if it does hold on to material.

11...   **Qb5**

12.Nb3   **Bg4**

13.Qd2

Now White loses material after a simple combination.

13...	Bxh2+!
14.Kxh2	Qxf1
15.Qf4	Bf3!
16.gxf3	

16.Qg3 Ng4+ 17.Kh3 Qh1+

16...	Qxf2+
17.Kh1	exf3
18.Qh2	

18.Qg5 Ne4 19.Qg1 Ng3+

18...	Qe1+

and here White resigned because if 19.Qg1, then 19...f2 wins. 0-1.

Black plays 3...Bc5 and White doesn't castle
Gilezetdinov–Tolush
Correspondence, 1970

1.e4 e5 2.Nf3 Nc6 3.Bb5 Bc5

This move order gives White some options at his 4th turn, but there is nothing to be afraid of.

4.c3	Nf6
5.d4	Bb6
6.Nxe5!?	

6.Qe2! is stronger.

6...	Nxe5
7.dxe5	Nxe4
8.Qg4	Bxf2+
9.Ke2?!	

9.Kd1!? Qh4 10.Qxg7 Rf8 11.b4 with the idea of Bh6 (11.Bh6?! Bc5 12.Rf1 Nf2+ 13.Rxf2 Qxf2 14.Nd2 Qf5! ∓) 11...Qh5+ (11...f6? 12.e6! Qh5+ 13.Kc2 ±) 12.Kc2 Qg6 (12...Bh4!? 13.Bh6 Be7 14.Rf1 b6! 15.e6

Nd6 led to unclear complications in Ree–Zuidema, Holland 1962.)
13.Qxg6 fxg6 and here Euwe claims that White stands better.

9...	**Qh4**
10.Qxg7	**Rf8**
11.Nd2!	

11.Bh6?! Bc5 12.Rf1 c6 13.Rf4 Qh5+ 14.Ke1 cxb5 15.Rxe4 b6 and
Black was clearly better in Florian–Forintos, Budapest 1961.

11.b4? f6! ∓

| **11...** | **Bc5?!** |

11...Nxd2 12.Bxd2 Bc5 13.Rhf1 Qe4+ (After 13...c6 Short–Gulko,
Linares 1989 ended in a draw.) 14.Kd1 Qg6 Black's lack of development
is not important here. 15.Qxg6 fxg6 16.Rxf8+ Bxf8 The position is level,
but Black has an easier time picking a target–the weak pawn at e5. Still,
the game will probably end in a draw.

| **12.Nf3** | **Qh5** |

12...Qf2+ 13.Kd1 Be7 14.Re1 Qb6! 15.Bc4?! Nc5 16.Be3 ±

| **13.Re1** | |

13.Rd1 would have been better, but the complications still favor
Black. 13...b6!? 14.Bd3 d5 15.exd6 Nxd6 16.Qe5+ Qxe5+ 17.Nxe5 Bb7
and I think that Black's position is to be preferred, once he castles.

| **13...** | **b6** |
| **14.Kf1** | **Bb7** |

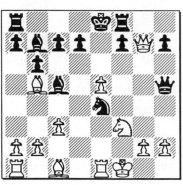

15.e6

15.Qh6 Qg4 leaves the situation quite unclear.

| **15...** | **0-0-0!** |

Now that the Black monarch has reached a safe haven it is White
who must worry about the safety of his king.

| **16.exd7+** | **Kb8** |

17.Qe5	Qg6
18.Nh4	Qg4
19.Qf4	

19.Nf3 Rxd7 20.Bxd7 Ba6+ 21.Re2 Bxe2+ 22.Kxe2 Qxg2+ 23.Kd3 Qxf3+ 24.Kc2 Rd8-+

19...	f5
20.Nf3	

20.Qxg4 fxg4+ 21.Ke2 Rf2+ 22.Kd1 c6 23.Rxe4 Rxd7+ 24.Ke1 cxb5 25.Bf4+ Kc8 26.Re8+ Rd8 27.Rxd8+ Kxd8 28.Rd1+ Ke8 ∓

20...	Bd6
21.Qh6	

21.Qxg4 fxg4 -+

21...	a6
22.Bd3	Rxd7
23.Re2	Rf6
24.Qe3	Bc5
25.Nd4	Bxd4
26.cxd4	

26...	Rxd4!
27.h3	

27.Qxd4 Nd2+ 28.Bxd2 Qxd4

27...	Qh4
28.Re1	Rxd3 0-1.

Martineav–Saavedra
Dubai Olympiad, 1986

1.e4 e5 2.Nf3 Nc6 3.Bb5 Bc5 4.b4

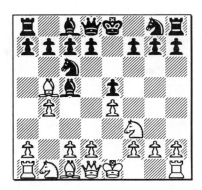

This is not an Evans Gambit! The pawn sacrifice is completely unsound, but does lead to complicated positions. Watch your back!

4...   **Nxb4**

I prefer this to the standard capture with the bishop. Especially since some misguided analysts consider it dubious!

5.c3

a) 5.Nxe5 Qe7 6.d4 c6 7.Bc4 d5 8.c3 dxc4 9.dxc5 (9.cxb4 Bxb4+ 10.Bd2 f6) Qxe5 10.cxb4 Qxa1-+

b) 5.Bb2 c6 6.Bc4 d5! (not the wimpy 6...d6 7.c3 Na6 8.d4 exd4 9.cxd4, when 9...Bb4+ can be met by 10.Kf1 with some compensation.) 7.exd5 Bf5! with a strong initiative for Black.

5...   **Nc6**
6d4

6.Bxc6 dxc6 7.Nxe5 Qe7 8.d4 Bd6 ∓

6.0-0 Nf6 7.d4 Bb6 8.dxe5 Nxe4 =. White has compensation for the pawn, but no more.

6...   **exd4**
7.0-0   **d3!**

This accomplishes the important goal of not allowing White to occupy d4 with his pawn.

8.Bc4

8.Qxd3 Nge7 9.c4 a6 10.Ba4 Nb4 and Black has the initiative.

8...   **d6**
9.Re1   **Be6**
10.Bxe6   **fxe6**
11.Qb3

11.Qxd3 Nf6 and White has no compensation for the pawn.

11...   **Qc8!**
12.e5   **d5**

13.c4	Nge7
14.Nc3	

14.Qxd3 might as well have been played here.

14...	0-0
15.cxd5	

White no doubt expected a prosaic recapture at d5 here. No such luck!

15...	Rxf3!
16.gxf3	

16.dxc6 Rxf2 17.Kh1 (17.Ne4 Rb2+) Qf8! followed by d2.

16...	Nd4
17.Qd1	exd5
18.Be3	Qh3
19.Bxd4	

Forced.

19...	Bxd4
20.Qxd3	

White finally recaptures the pawn, but his kingside is a shambles.

20...	Nf5
21.Kh1	Bxf2
22.Qxd5+	Kh8
23.Rg1	Ng3+!
24.Rxg3	Bxg3
25.Qd2	Bxh2

25...Bxe5 might have been even simpler.

26.Qxh2	Qxf3+
27.Qg2	Qxc3

And the rest was just a matter of not falling into any traps.

28.Rg1 Qxe5 29.Qxb7 Rd8 30.Rb1 h6 31.Qg2 Rd4 32.Rb8+ Kh7 33.Qc2+ g6 34.Qf2 Qd5+ 0-1.

The Hungarian Defence to the Italian Game

(1.e4 e5 2.Nf3 Nc6 3.Bc4 d6)

Ziulyarkin–Karpov
Zlatoust, 1962

1.e4 e5 2.Nf3 Nc6 3.Bc4 Be7

The Hungarian Defense is a viable alternative to the Two Knights Defense or Italian Game. It is very solid and conforms to opening principles.

4.d4	**d6**
5.c3	

This move is not in ECO but it is a logical way of supporting the center.

5...	**Nf6**
6.dxe5	

6.Qe2 Bg4 puts a lot of pressure on White's center.

6...	**Nxe5**
7.Nxe5	**dxe5**
8.Qc2	

8.Qxd8+ Bxd8 gives White nothing, as we shall see in other games.

8...	**0-0**
9.Bg5	**c6**
10.Bxf6?!	

A completely unmotivated exchange of B for N.

10...	Bxf6
11.Nd2	Qe7
12.0-0-0	

This invites a queenside attack, and Karpov is willing to oblige.

12...	b5
13.Be2	Be6
14.Kb1	Rab8
15.g4	c5
16.h4	

The kingside pawnstorm cannot be effective because Black has not advanced any pawns in that area and has no weaknesses to attack.

16...	Qc7
17.g5	Be7
18.c4	

18.Rdg1 Qa5 19.c4 Rfd8 20.Nb3 Qb4 21.cxb5 c4! 22.Nc1 Rd2 23.Qc3 Qxc3 24.bxc3 Rxb5+ 25.Ka1 Ba3-+

18...	a6
19.Ka1	Rb6
20.Nf1	bxc4
21.Ne3	Re8

To make room for the bishop to retreat. 21...Rfb8 would have made more sense.

22.Bxc4	Bxc4
23.Nxc4	Rb4
24.Rd5	f6
25.gxf6	Bxf6
26.a3	Rbb8
27.Nd6?	

A mistake, since the knight occupied an effective post at c4.

| 27... | Red8 |
| 28.Qc4 | |

This seem to create major threats on the diagonal.

28...	Kf8!
29.Rhd1	Qb6

Now White must have really wished the knight were still at c4!

30.R5d2??

30.R1d2 Bxh4 31.Qa2 Qb3 32.Qxb3 Rxb3 33.Rxe5 Rb6 34.Nc4 Rxd2 35.Nxd2 Bf6 36.Nc4 Bxe5 37.Nxb6 Bd4∓

30...Rxd6 31.b4 Rxd2 32.Rxd2 cxb4 33.Rd7 Be7 34.a4 b3 35.Kb1 Qxf2 0-1

Mestel–Smyslov
Las Palmas Interzonal, 1982

1.e4 e5 2.Nf3 Nc6 3.Bc4 Be7 4.d4 d6 5.d5 Nb8

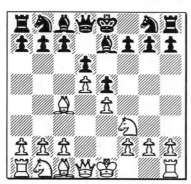

This is considered the main line by ECO. White's bishop now looks awkward and Black can obtain counterplay with f7–f5.

6.Bd3

6.Bb5+ c6 7.dxc6 bxc6 8.Bc4 Nf6 9.Nc3 0-0 10.0-0 Nbd7 11.Qe2 a5 12.Rd1 Qc7= Filipowicz–Ciocaltea, Halle 1974.

6...	Nf6
7.c4	

7.h3 c6 8.c4 b5! 9.Nc3 b4 10.Ne2 0-0 11.Be3 cxd5! 12.cxd5 Na6= Δ Nc5.

7...	0-0
8.Nc3	

8.h3 Nbd7 (8...Ne8!?) 9.Nc3 Ne8 10.0-0 g6 11.Bh6 Ng7 12.Qd2± is probably the best White can hope for, Fuchs–Kholmov, Leningrad 1967.

8...	c6
9.0-0	Nbd7

| 10.Rb1 | Re8 |
| 11.b4 | Nf8 |

Black is playing solidly, waiting for his opponent to overextend.

| 12.Re1 | Ng6 |
| 13.Bf1 | Rf8! |

Smyslov returns to the plan of f7–f5.

| 14.Qb3 | Kh8 |
| 15.Bb2 | |

15.dxc6 bxc6 16.b5 Bg4 is unclear, according to Smyslov.

15...	cxd5
16.cxd5	Ng4
17.h3	Nh6
18.Rbc1	f5
19.Nb5	

19.exf5 Bxf5 20.Ne4 Nf4∓

19...	fxe4
20.Rxe4	Bf5
21.Rec4	

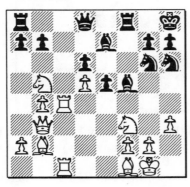

| 21... | Nh4! |
| 22.Nxh4 | |

22.Nc7 Rc8 23.Nxh4 Bxh4 24.g3 Bg5 25.Ne6 Bxe6 26.dxe6 Bxc1 27.Bxc1 Rxc4 28.Bxc4 Nf5∓

| 22... | Bxh4 |
| 23.g3 | |

23.Nxd6? Bxf2+ 24.Kxf2 Bc2+!

23...Bg5 24.Rd1 Qb6!∓ 25.h4 Ng4! 26.Rdd4 Bh6 27.Nc7 Rac8 28.Ne6 Bxe6 29.dxe6 Rce8

White's position is now hopeless.

30.Be2 Nxf2 31.Rd5 Nh3+ 32.Kg2 Qg1+ 33.Kxh3 Qh1+ 34.Kg4 Qxd5 35.Rf4 Rxf4+ 0-1

Rogers–Ivkov
Bor, 1984

**1.e4 e5 2.Nf3 Nc6 3.Bc4 Be7 4.d4 d6 5.dxe5 dxe5 6.Qxd8+
Bxd8**

The early exchange of queens does not bring White any advantage.

7.Bd5

7.Ng5 Bxg5 8.Bxg5 Nd4! 9.Na3 Be6= Szabo-Znosko-Borovsky, Zaandam 1946. Black's initiative compensates for the bishop pair.

7.Nc3 Nf6 8.Be3 Bg4!? (8...Be7 9.Nd5± Van der Wiel–Nikolíc, Malta Olympiad 1980.) 9.0-0-0 a6 looks quite playable for Black.

7...	**Nge7!?**
8.Bb3	**f6**
9.c3	

Otherwise the bishop has no place to go when attacked by Black's knight.

9...	**Na5**
10.Ba4+?!	

This just helps Black, since the king finds a save haven on f7.

10...	**Kf7!**
11.Nbd2	**Be6**
12.b4	**Nc4**
13.Nxc4	**Bxc4∓**

White has a weak pawn structure, and Black's position is just fine.

14.Bb3	**Be6!**
15.Bxe6+	**Kxe6**
16.a4	

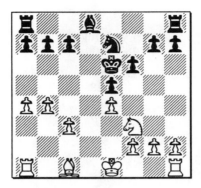

The centralized king is in no danger, and Black is well-prepared for the endgame. Now he just needs to untangle his pieces.

	16...	Nc8!
	17.Be3	a5
	18.Ke2	Be7

White's advanced queenside pawns are easy targets.

	19.Rhb1	Nd6
	20.Nd2	b6
	21.f3	g6
	22.b5	Rhd8
	23.Rd1	Nb7
	24.c4	Rac8

24...Nc5 25.Bxc5 Bxc5 26.Nb3=

	25.Nb3	Rxd1
	26.Rxd1	Bb4
	27.c5?!	

This must have been a miscalculation by Rogers, but his position was getting very passive and f6–f5 was coming.

	27...	bxc5
	28.Rc1	

28...	c6!
29.b6	

29.Nxc5+ Nxc5 30.Bxc5 cxb5∓

29.Bxc5! cxb5 30.Bxb4 Rxc1 31.Nxc1 axb4 32.axb5 Kd6 33.Nd3 b3 34.Kd2 Nc5 35.Nxc5 b2 36.Nb7+ Kc7 37.Kc2 Kxb7 38.Kxb2 Kb6 39.Kb3 Kxb5

29.bxc6 Rxc6

29...	c4!
30.Nd2	

30.Rxc4 c5 and the b-pawn falls.

30...	Bxd2
31.Bxd2	c5
32.f4	Rd8!
33.fxe5	fxe5
34.Rf1	Rd4
35.Bg5	

35.Ke3 Nd6

35...	Rxe4+
36.Kd1	c3
37.Rf6+	Kd5
38.Rf7	Nd6
39.Rxh7	Rxa4
40.Bd8	

40.b7 Rb4

40...	Rb4-+
41.Bc7 0-1	

Roos–Ivkov
Baden Baden, 1981

1.e4 e5 2.Nf3 Nc6 3.Bc4 Be7 4.d4 d6 5.dxe5 dxe5 6.Bd5

An attempt to avoid the early exchange of queens.

6...	**Bd7**
7.0-0	**Nf6**
8.Nc3	**Bd6!**
9.Re1	

9.Bg5 h6 10.Bh4 g5 11.Bg3 Qe7 and White may be in trouble on the kingside.

9...	**h6**
10.a4	**0-0**
11.Nb5	**a6**
12.Na3	

12.Nxd6 cxd6 will not bring an advantage since Black can place a great deal of pressure on the d5-square and use the semi-open c-file.

12...	**Qe7**
13.Nc4	**Rfd8!**

Although there are many pieces sitting on the d-file, the rook occupies the best position it can find.

14.Qe2	**Qe8**
15.c3	**Be6**
16.Bxe6	**Qxe6**
17.b4	**Bf8**
18.Rb1	**Nd7**

Black is on the defensive, but his game is easy to play.

19.h3	**Ne7**
20.Ne3	**Nf6**
21.Qc4	

Black's control of d5 has prevented White from placing a knight there. Now the position explodes into a tactical melee.

21...	**Rd6!**

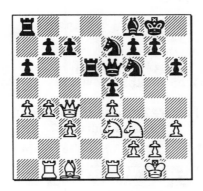

21...Qxc4? 22.Nxc4±.

	22.Qxc7

22.Qxe6 Rxe6 23.Nc4 Ng6 =.

22...	Rc8
23.Qa5	

23.Qxb7 Rd7.

23...	Nc6
24.Qc5	Rd1!
25.Qc4	

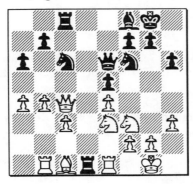

25...	Nd4!!
26.Qf1	Nxf3+
27.gxf3	Rxe1
28.Qxe1	Qxh3∓
29.Qe2	

White realizes that the pawn at f3 is more important than the one at c3, but Black has more ambitious plans than mere material gain.

29...	Nh5!
30.Ng4	Rxc3

31.Be3	**Nf4**
32.Bxf4	

32.Qf1 Qxf3 33.Nh2 Nh3+.

32...exf4 33.Nh2 Rc6 34.Kh1 Bxb4! 35.Rg1 Bf8 36.Qd2 Qh4 37.Rg4 Qf6 38.Rg1 h5 39.Rb1 b6 40.Qd5 g6 0-1

Paoli (2220)–Medancic (2320)
Reggio Emilia, 1987

1.e4 e5 2.Nf3 Nc6 3.Bc4 Be7 4.d4 d6 5.h3

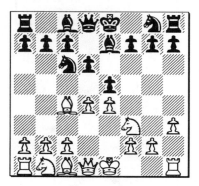

This is just too slow.

5...	**Nf6**

5...Nxd4!? 6.Nxd4 exd4 7.Qh5 g6 8.Qd5 Be6 9.Qxb7 Nf6! 10.Bxe6 fxe6 11.Qc6+ Kf7 12.Nd2 Qd7 brought Black equality in Sax–Ivkov, Amsterdam 1976.

6.Nc3	**0-0**

The game has transposed into a Four Knights where White has played the useless h2–h3.

7.0-0!?

7.Bg5 h6 =.

7...	**Nxe4**
8.Nxe4	**d5**
9.Bxd5	**Qxd5**
10.Nc3	**Qa5**
11.d5	**Rd8**

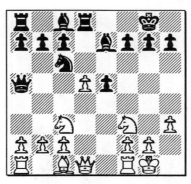

12.Qe2	Nb4
13.Nxe5	Bf6!

There is no need to hastily regain the pawn.

14.Nc4	Qa6
15.Ne4	Be7
16.Nc3	Bf8
17.Bg5	f6
18.Be3	Nxd5

Finally the pawn is recaptured, and Black has the bishop pair and a solid position, since White lacks a light-squared bishop to act on the weakened a2–g8 diagonal.

19.Nxd5	Rxd5∓
20.b3	

This creates a weakness, but the pin had to be broken.

20...	Be6
21.Qf3	

21.Rfd1 Rad8.

21...	Rf5
22.Qe4	Re8!
23.Nb2	Ra5
24.Qd3	

24.a4 Bf7∓

24...	Qc6
25.c4	Rh5
26.Qe2	

26...Rxh3!! 27.gxh3 Bxh3 28.f3 Rxe3! 29.Qxe3 Bc5 30.Kh2 Bxe3 31.Kxh3 Qd7+ 32.Kg3 Qd4-+ 33.Na4 Qf4+ 34.Kg2 Qg5+ 35.Kh3 h5

There is no stopping h5–h4 and Qg3+. 0-1

The Scotch Game

(1.e4 e5 2.Nf3 Nc6 3.d4)
Karlsen–Barkhagen
Gausdal, 1991

1.e4 e5 2.Nf3 Nc6 3.d4 exd4 4.Bc4

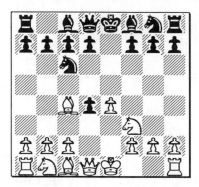

The Scotch Gambit is an enterprising opening which is popular at the club level. It must be handled with care.

| 4... | d6!? |

This is not the most aggressive option for Black, but it leads to a fully playable game without the risk of the main lines.

| 5.Nxd4 | Be7 |

This move order avoids nuisance pins at g5.

| 6.Nc3 | Nf6 |
| 7.f3 | |

7.Bg5 Nxe4 8.Bxe7 Nxc3 9.Bxd8 Nxd1 10.Nxc6 Nxb2! 11.Bb5 bxc6 12.Bxc6+ Kxd8 13.Bxa8 Re8+ 14.Kd2 Nc4+ 15.Kc3∞

| 7... | 0-0 |
| 8.Be3 | a6 |

White's formation looks artificial. This system works against the Dragon but the B at c4 is vulnerable and a kingside attack is unlikely to succeed since Black has not weakened his kingside pawn structure.

| 9.Qd2 | Ne5 |
| 10.Be2 | |

10.Bb3 b5 creates the deadly threat of c7–c5–c4.

| 10... | d5! |

11.exd5	Nxd5
12.0-0-0	Nxe3
13.Qxe3	

13...	Ng4!
14.Qg1	

14.fxg4?? Bg5.

14...	Bg5+
15.Kb1	Be3
16.Qe1	Bf2

16...Bxd4 17.fxg4 Bxc3 18.Qxc3 Qe7 19.Rhe1 Be6 =.

17.Qd2	Ne3
18.Ne4	

18.Rc1 Nxg2

18...	Nxd1
19.Rxd1	Qxd4
20.Qxd4	Bxd4
21.Rxd4∓	

Black has emerged with an extra exchange.

21...Bf5 22.Ng3 Be6 23.b3 Rad8 24.Re4 Rfe8 25.Bd3 Bd5 26.Rh4 g6 27.Rg4 Re1+ 28.Kb2 Be6 29.Rb4 Bc8 30.Be4 b5 31.Bd3 Rg1 32.Kc3 c5 33.Rh4 f5 34.f4 Be6 35.a4 b4+ 36.Kb2 Rxg2 37.Bxa6 Rdd2 0-1

Loedel–Barboza
Carrasco, 1921

**1.e4 e5 2.Nf3 Nc6 3.d4 exd4 4.Nxd4 d6 5.Nc3 Be7 6.Bc4 Nf6
7.a3**

This move is intended to secure lodging for the exposed cleric, but it gives the initiative to Black.

7...	Bg4!

8.f3	Bd7
9.Be3	a6!
10.Nce2	Ne5
11.Ba2	g6

11...c5 12.Nf5 Bxf5 13.exf5 d5 would have been more logical

12.Nf4	c6
13.0-0	Qc7
14.Rc1?!	

An incomprehensible move, but then Black's position was already solid enough to frustrate any ambitious plan by White.

| 14... | h5 |

This move takes control of g4.

15.c4	h4
16.Nd3	Nh5!?
17.Nxe5	dxe5
18.Ne2	g5∓
19.c5	Nf4
20.Nxf4	gxf4
21.Bd2	

21.Bf2 0-0-0 Δ f5.

| 21... | Rg8 |
| 22.Kf2 | |

An attempt to flee to safety, but Black will break through on the kingside anyway.

22...Rg7 23.b4 0-0-0 24.Qc2 Rdg8 25.Rg1 h3! 26.g3 fxg3+ 27.hxg3 h2! 28.Rg2 Bh3 29.Rxh2 Rxg3 30.Bxf7

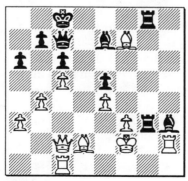

30...Rg2+ 31.Rxg2 Rxg2+ 0-1

The Ponziani Opening
(1.e4 e5 2.Nf3 Nc6 3.c3)

Makkropoulos–Tolnai
Dortmund, 1988
1.e4 e5 2.Nf3 Nc6 3.c3 d5 4.Qa4

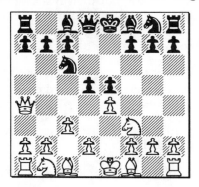

This is White's main alternative.

4...	**Bd7**

A sensible reply which leads to a simplification of the position.

5.exd5	**Nd4**
6.Qd1	**Nxf3+**
7.Qxf3	**Nf6**

7...Bd6!? is an interesting alternative: 8.Bc4 f5 9.d3 Qf6 with a very solid position for Black.

8.Bc4

8.c4 Bc5 leaves White very weak on the dark squares.

8.d4? exd4 9.cxd4 Qe7+! 10.Be3? Qb4+ ∓ Hofstatter–Rapp, Switzerland 1968.

8...	**e4!**

The most aggressive continuation.

9.Qe2

9.Qg3 Bd6! 10.Qxg7 Rg8 ∓–Khristov.

9...	**Bd6!?**

9...Qe7 is also good, intending to castle queenside.

10.d4	**0-0**
11.h3	**Re8**

12.Be3	h6
13.Nd2	

Black has a comfortable game.

13...	Nh7

13...Qe7 is a reasonable alternative.

14.0-0-0	f5
15.g3	Nf6
16.f4	

Pretty much forced, in order to stop the kingside onslaught. But now Black can turn his attention elsewhere.

16...	a6
17.Rdg1	b5
18.Bb3	a5
19.a3	h5!

Black is careful to take time out to defend the kingside.

20.c4	a4
21.Ba2	bxc4
22.Nxc4	Bb5

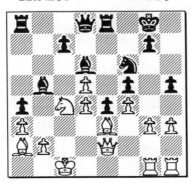

Black has a dominating position, so White decides to go for broke.

23.g4	hxg4
24.hxg4	fxg4
25.Rh4	Qd7
26.Qh2	Bxc4
27.Bxc4	Qf5!

From this vantage point the Black queen both defends the kingside and puts pressure at d5.

28.Be2	Qxd5
29.Rhxg4	

29.Rh8+ Kf7 achieves nothing for White.

29...	Nxg4
30.Rxg4	Qb3
31.Qh6	Re7
32.f5	Rf7
33.f6	Bf8
34.d5	

White hopes that one day the bishop will reach the a1–h8 diagonal, but this absorbs too much time.

34...	Qxd5
35.Qh4	Re8
36.Bd2	Re6
37.Bc3	

Finally, but the bishop will be ineffective once it is pinned.

37...	Rc6
38.fxg7	Bxg7
39.Rxe4	

39...	Rff6!

A beautiful and subtle move which brings the game to a rapid conclusion. The threat is simply Rh6.

40.Re8+		Rf8	
41.Rxf8+		Kxf8	0-1.

The Three Knights Opening

(1.e4 e5 2.Nf3 Nc6 3.Nc3)

Orlov–Mitkov
Leningrad, 1991

1.e4 e5 2.Nf3 Nc6 3.Nc3

The Three Knights is a slow opening that usually transposes elsewhere, but a recent game may show that a line thought to be bad for Black is really quite playable!

3...	Bc5

This is considered bad because White can capture at e5.

4.Nxe5	Nxe5
5.d4	

5...	Bd6
6.dxe5	Bxe5
7.f4	

7.Nd5?! c6 8.Ne3 Nf6 9.Bc4 0-0 10.Qd3 Re8 led to unclear complications in a game from the Paulsen–Anderssen match of 1877, but Black has a solid position with no weaknesses, and White has no real kingside attack.

7.Bd3 Bxc3+ 8.bxc3 d6 9.0-0 Nf6=

7...	Bxc3+
8.bxc3	Nf6
9.e5	

<table>
<tr><td>**9...**</td><td>**Ne4!?**</td></tr>
</table>

9...Qe7 is the only move given in ECO. 10.Be2 Ne4 11.Qd4 f5 12.Bf3 Qc5 13.Bxe4 Qxd4 14.cxd4 fxe4 15.d5 b6 16.Bb2 Bb7 17.0-0-0± which dates back to the Bilguer Handbuch!

10.Qf3

10.Qd4 f5 11.Bd3 c5 12.Qd5 Qh4+!

10...	d5
11.Bd3	Qh4+
12.g3	Qh3!

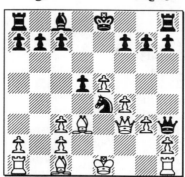

13.c4

13.Bxe4 Bg4 14.Qg2 dxe4 15.Qxe4 0-0-0 16.Bd2 Bf5 with aggressive compensation for Black.

13...	Bg4
14.Qf1	Nc5
15.Be2	Qxf1+
16.Bxf1	

16.Rxf1 Bxe2 17.Kxe2 dxc4 18.Be3 Na6 is about level, with White having compensation for the pawn, but no more.

16...	Bf3
17.Rg1	0-0-0
18.Ba3	Ne6
19.cxd5	Bxd5
20.Bd3	

20...	Nd4!
21.Kf2	Nf3
22.Bf5+	Kb8
23.Rgd1	Bc6
24.h3	

24.Bg4 Nxh2

24...	g6
25.Bd3	Rd7
26.g4	Rhd8
27.Kg3	h5!

This opens up a critical file.

28.gxh5

28.g5 h4+ 29.Kg4?? Rh8would be very embarassing!

28...	gxh5
29.Be2	Nd4!
30.Bd3	Rg8+

Black uses the open file to great effect.

31.Kh4

31.Kf2 Rg2+32.Ke3 Rg3+ 33.Kf2 Rxh3∓

31...Rg2 32.Bf8 Rd8 33.Bh6 f6! 34.Bg5

(34.Bf1 Nf3+35.Kxh5 Be8+#) and White resigned before

34...fxg5+ 35.fxg5 Nf3+ 36.Kxh5 Rxg5+ 37.Kh6 Rxe5 etc. **0-1**

Bishop's Opening

(1.e4 e5 2. Bc4)

Inkiov–Belyavsky
Novi Sad Olympiad, 1990
1.e4 e5 2.Bc4

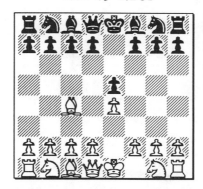

The Bishop's Opening is recommended in the companion volume on an opening repertoire for White. It is not all that easy to meet.

2...   Nf6
3.d3

In the companion volume 3.d4!? is recommended as a more aggressive line.

3...   c6
4.Nf3

4.Bg5 d5! 5.exd5 cxd5 6.Bb5+ Nc6 is fine for Black, Asharin–Vogt, Tartu 1964.

4.f4 exf4 5.Bxf4 d5 6.exd5 Nxd5 7.Qf3 Nxf4 8.Qxf4 Bb4+! 9.c3 Qe7+ 10.Ne2 Bd6 is also good for Black (adapting an idea from ECO).

4.Bb3 Bc5 5.Nf3 d6 is similar to the Hungarian Defense, and should be fine for Black.

4.Qe2 Be7 5.Nf3 0-0 6.Bb3 d5 7.Nbd2 Nbd7 8.c3 Qc7= Wade–Teschner, Hastings 1953/54.

4...   Be7!?

An interesting alternative to the normal 4...d5.

5.Bb3   0-0
6.0-0

6.Nxe5?? is a blunder that is swiftly punished by Qa5+

6...	d6
7.Nbd2	Nbd7
8.c3	

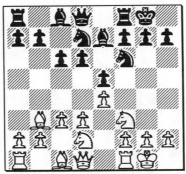

Now that the initial development is complete, Black can expand in the center.

8...	d5
9.Re1	Qc7
10.exd5!?	

10.Nf1 is very passive. 10...Nc5 11.Bc2 dxe4 12.dxe4 Rd8 13.Qe2 b6! and the a6-square is inviting.

| 10... | cxd5 |
| 11.c4 | d4! |

11...dxc4? 12.Nxc4±

11...Bc5 12.cxd5 Qb6 13.Rf1 Ng4 14.Ne4±

           12.Nf1

12.Nxd4!? Nc5!? (12...exd4 13.Rxe7 Qd6 14.Re1 Nc5 15.Nf1 Bf5

16.Bc2±) 13.Nb5 Qd8 14.Rxe5 Nxd3 gives Black a strong initiative, and the Bb3 is pathetic.

12...	**Bb4**

12...b6? is premature because of 13.Nxd4!

13.Bd2	**Bxd2**
14.Qxd2	**b6!**

Now it is playable.

15.Ng3	**Bb7**
16.Nh4	**Nc5**

16...g6!? comes into consideration.

17.Qg5!	**Nfd7**

17...Nxd3 18.Ngf5 Ne8 19.c5! Δ Nxe1 20.Ne7+ Kh8 allows 21.Nhg6+!!+-

18.Ngf5	**Ne6**
19.Qg3	**g6**

20.c5!	**Ndxc5**
21.Bxe6	**Nxe6**

21...fxe6 22.Nh6+ Kh8 23.Ng4±

22.Rac1	**Qd8**
23.Nh6+	**Kh8**
24.Qxe5+	**Ng7**

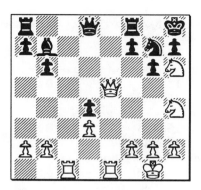

This is a critical position.

25.Qe7?!

25.Rc7! Bd5 26.Re7 Re8 27.Qf6 Rxe7 28.Rxe7 Rc8 29.h3 (29.Nxf7+ Bxf7 30.Qxf7?? Rc1+) Rc7 30.Rxf7!? Rc1+ 31.Kh2 Qb8+ 32.Qf4 Qxf4+ 33.Rxf4 Ne6 and Black's active pieces give him counterplay for the pawn.

25.Qf4!? Bd5 26.Nf3 might allow an infiltration at g5. 26...Bxf3

a) 27.Nxf7+ Kg8 (27...Rxf7 28.Qxf7 Bd5!?) 28.Nh6+ Kh8 29.Nf7+=;

b) 27.Qxf3

25.Nf3 f6 26.Qc7∞

25...	Bd5
26.a3	Re8
27.Qxd8	Raxd8

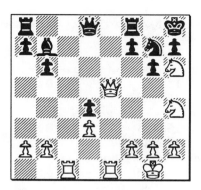

28.g4?!

28.Nf3!? might have been better.

28...	Rxe1+
29.Rxe1	Re8

30.Rc1

30.Rxe8+ Nxe8

30...   f6!

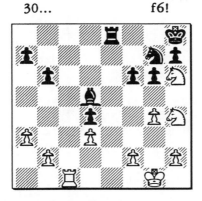

The White knights now look silly.

31.Ng2	Ne6
32.Nf7+	Kg7
33.Nd6	Rd8
34.Nb5?	

34.Ne4 is more promising here: 34...f5 35.gxf5 gxf5 36.Ng3 Bxg2 37.Kxg2 Nf4+ 38.Kf3 Nxd3 39.Nxf5+ Kf6∓

34...   Rd7!

There is no good defense now for White.

35.a4	Bxg2
36.Kxg2	Nf4+
37.Kf1	Nxd3
38.Rc4	

38.Rc2 a6 39.Na3 Nc5 40.a5 d3 41.Rc1 Nb3

38...	Nxb2
39.Rb4	d3!
40.Rxb2	d2
41.Nc3	d1Q+
42.Nxd1	Rxd1+
43.Kg2	

43.Ke2 Rd5! and Black wins the rook endgame.

43...   Rd5

43...Rd4? 44.a5!

44.Rb5?!   Rd4

And White resigned because of 45.a5 Rxg4+ 46.Kf3 Rg5 0-1

Knorr–Langheld
Correspondence, 1990

1.e4 e5 2.Bc4 Nf6 3.d4

This is the move I recommend for White.

3...	exd4
4.Nf3	Nxe4
5.Qxd4	Nf6
6.Bg5	Be7
7.Nc3	Nc6
8.Qh4	d6

8...d5 9.0-0-0 Be6 10.Rhe1 0-0 11.Bd3 h6 12.Rxe6 fxe6 13.Bxh6 gxh6 14.Qg3+ Kh8 15.Qg6 Bb4 16.Qxh6+ Kg8 17.Qg6+ 1/2 Leisebein–Markus, corr. 1989

9.0-0-0	**Be6!**

This recent innovation improves on a century-old game!

9...Bf5 10.Rhe1 0-0 11.Qf4 Bg6 12.g4 gives White a strong attack, Keidanski–Lasker, Berlin 1891.

10.Bd3	Qd7
11.Bb5	0-0

12.Ne5

An attempt to exploit all of the pins.

12...   **Qe8**

12...Qc8 13.Nxc6 bxc6 14.Bxc6 h6 15.Be3 Nd5 16.Qg3 Nxe3 17.Qxe3 Rb8 with counterplay. Leisebein–Thielen, corr. 1989/90

13.Nxc6   **bxc6**
14.Bd3   **h6**

All of a sudden White's pressure is dissipating.

15.f4?!

15.Bxh6 was clearly the right move. 15...Ng4 16.Bg5 Bxg5+ 17.Qxg5 f6 and I rather doubt Black has anything to worry about on the kingside, though there might be some action on the h-file. 18.Qf4 Qf7 19.h4 Ne5 20.h5 Bxa2 gets pretty wild.

15...   **Nd5!**
16.Nxd5   **Bxg5!**
17.fxg5   **Bxd5**
18.gxh6

White must have missed Black's next move.

18...	Qe3+!
19.Rd2	Qxh6
20.Qxh6	gxh6

Black has all the chances in this endgame.

21.c4 Be6 22.Be4 Bd7 23.Re1 Rae8 24.Rde2 Re6 25.Bf3 Rfe8 26.Kc2 Rxe2+ 27.Rxe2 Rxe2+ 28.Bxe2-+

The bishop endgame is really just a matter of technique.

28...c5 29.Bf3 Kg7 30.h4 f5 31.Kd2 Kf6 32.b3 Ke5 33.Kc1

33.Ke3 f4+ 34.Kd3 Bf5+ 35.Kc3 Be4

33...f4 34.Kb2 Kd4 35.h5 c6 36.Kc1 d5 37.cxd5 cxd5 38.Kb2 Bf5 0-1

King's Gambit

(1.e4 e5 2.f4)

Illescas–Murey
Holon, 1987

1.e4 e5 2.f4 d5

If White wants to play a gambit, why not offer a countergambit? The Falkbeer has a lot of interesting byways. We are going to examine one of them.

3.exd5

Here the normal move is 3...e4 while 3...c6 has been popular. But Black can also head into the paths of the Modern variation, sidestepping annoyances like the Bishop's Gambit, Breyer, and other divergences.

3.Nf3 exf4 4.exd5 transposes below.

3...	**exf4**
4.Nf3	**Nf6**
5.Bb5+	

The most dangerous for Black, according to Korchnoi & Zak (1986).

a) 5.Bc4 Bd6 6.Nc3 0-0 7.0-0 c6 8.d4 cxd5 9.Nxd5 Be6 10.Nxf6+ Qxf6 11.Bxe6 (11.Be2 Korchnoi & Zak consider this position more attractive for White, but I am not sure why. Nc6 and Black will put his rooks in the center, with strong pressure. He can also look to the kingside for attacking possibilities.) 11...fxe6 12.Ne5 Bxe5 13.dxe5 Qxe5 14.Bxf4 Qc5+ 15.Kh1 Nc6 =. Bronstein–Matanovic, Lvov 1962.

b) 5.Nc3 Bd6 6.Bb5+ (6.Bc4—5.Bc4.) Nbd7 7.Qe2+ Qe7 8.Qxe7+

Kxe7 9.0-0 Rd8 10.d4 Nb6 11.Bd2 Bf5 12.Ne1 Kf8 =. Pomar–Medina, Las Palmas 1974.

c) 5.c4 c6 6.d4 cxd5 7.c5 Nc6 8.Bxf4 Be7 9.Nc3 0-0 10.Bb5 Ne4 11.0-0 Bg4 12.Qa4 Bxf3 13.gxf3 (13.Rxf3 Nxd4 14.Qxd4 Bxc5) Ng5 14.Bg3 Ne6 with a comfortable game for Black, Tolush–Averbakh, Leningrad 1959.

5...   **c6**

5...Bd7 6.Be2!? Bd6 7.c4 0-0 8.d4 c5 9.0-0 Re8 10.Kh1 Na6 11.Nc3 b6 12.Bd3 h6 13.Bc2 g5 ∞. Van der Plassche–Scheeren, Eindhoven 1987

6.dxc6   **Nxc6**
7.d4   **Bd6**
8.Qe2+

8.0-0 0-0 9.Nbd2 (9.c3 Nd5! =.) Bg4 10.Nc4 Bc7 11.Bxc6 bxc6 12.Qd3 Qd5 (Glaskov–Simitsyn, USSR 1972) 13.Nfe5 Here Korchnoi claims an advantage for White. 13...Bh5 14.Bxf4 Rfe8 This is a very complicated position, but the bishop pair and central pressure are probably worth the pawn.

8...   **Kf8!?**

A novelty, introduced in this game.

8...Be6 9.Ng5 0-0 10.Nxe6 fxe6 11.Bxc6 bxc6 12.0-0 ∞.

9.Bxc6?   **bxc6**
10.Ne5   **Qb6!**
11.Nc4!?

11.c3 Ba6 ∓

11...Qxd4 12.Nxd6 Qxd6 13.0-0 g5 14.Bd2 Qc5+ 15.Kh1 Bg4 16.Qe1 Kg7 17.Bb4 Qf5 18.Qc3 Rhe8 19.Nd2 Kg8 20.Rae1 Be2 21.Rf2 Bb5 22.Rxe8+ Rxe8 23.h3 Re1+ 24.Kh2 g4 25.g3 Qd5! 0-1.

Vienna Game

(1.e4 e5 2.Nc3)

Meitner–L.Paulsen
Vienna, 1873

1.e4 e5 2.Nc3

The Vienna Game is unambitious, but not innocuous. If Black is not careful, it is easy to fall into reversed openings a tempo down. But if we keep in mind that this is a respectable, classical opening, there is no danger.

2...   **Bc5!?**

Most books dismiss this move with comments that suggest that White can do just about anything and get an advantage, but can always bail out into the Three Knights if necessary. It is a decent move with good surprise value.

3.Bc4

We have already seen examples of the Three Knights, which arises on 3.Nf3 Nc6. Konstantinopolsky & Lepeshkin, in their 1983 book on the Vienna, recommend that as the best line for White.

3.f4 d6! 4.Nf3 Nc6 5.Bc4 (5.Na4 Bb6 6.Nxb6 axb6 7.d3 Nf6 8.Be2 0-0 9.0-0 Re8 10.c3 Qe7 =. Alapin–Janowski, Prague 1908.) Bg4 6.h3 Bxf3 7.Qxf3 Nd4 8.Qg3 exf4! 9.Qxf4 Qf6 10.Qg3 Qg6 ∓ Spielmann–Albin, Vienna 1907.

3...   **Nc6**

4.d3

4.Qg4 g6 (4...Kf8!? is an interesting alternative. Konsantinopolski &

Lepeshkin give further: 5.Qf3 Nf6 6.Nge2 d6 7.d3 h6 8.h3 with a slightly better game for White, but I think that Black has little to worry about.) 5.Qf3 Nf6 6.Nge2 Bf8! Keres idea. Black will fianchetto the bishop and then castle with a solid position, especially since White's forces are not properly aligned for an attack, for example: 7.0-0 Bg7 8.d3 0-0 9.Bg5 h6 10.Be3 d6 11.h4 Be6 ∞.

4...	Na5!
5.Nf3	Nxc4
6.dxc4	d6

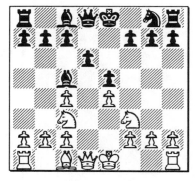

Already Black has a comfortable game.

7.Qd3	Ne7
8.Be3	Bxe3
9.Qxe3	b6
10.0-0-0	Nc6
11.Nd2	0-0
12.f3?!	Be6
13.g4	a6
14.b3	b5
15.Qd3	bxc4?!

15...b4! ∓

16.Nxc4 a5 17.a4 Nb4 18.Qe2 Qe7 19.Ne3 Rfb8 20.Ncd5 Nxd5 21.Nxd5 Qd8 Unfortunately I do not have the remainder of the moves of this game, but it is clear that Black is certainly no worse, and has definite chances on the queenside.

Miscellaneous Open Games

(1.e4 e5)

Von Lawaetz–Wittrup
Nordisk Skaktidende, 1876

1.e4 e5 2.d4 exd4 3.c3

This is the Danish Gambit, an old opening which can be quite dangerous for Black if caught unawares.

3...	dxc3
4.Bc4	cxb2

So many books advocate declining the gambit that acceptance may come as a surprise. If this move doesn't, then the next move certainly will.

5.Bxb2	Nh6!?

This is the Nordic Defense. With White's bishop off the c1–h6 diagonal, the knight is safe here and can guard f7. White has a number of replies here.

6.Ne2

A comfortable developing move which allows White to aim for f2–f4, but there are plenty of alternatives.

At one time 6.Nf3 was considered best, but Black did not find the best moves. 6...Bb4+ 7.Nc3 0-0 8.0-0 c6!? It is important that White not be allowed to use d5 as a pivot point for his knight. Here Black can place pressure on the e-pawn or return the pawn eventually by d7–d5, freeing his game. Practical tests are needed.

6.Nc3 b6 (6...Bb4 and even 6...b5!? come into consideration here) 7.Nf3 (7.Qe2 was recommended by V. Nielsen in 1877, as Black is aiming for Ba6. 7...Nc6 8.Nf3 Bb7 9.0-0 d6 White has some pressure for the pawn, but Black threatens to play Qd7 and then castle queenside with a solid position.)

a) 7...Bb7 8.Nd5! (8.Qc2 Na6 9.0-0-0 Nc5 10.Nd5 Ne6 gave Black a solid game in V.Nielsen–Delcomyn, Correspondence 1894–1895.) Bxd5 9.exd5 Bb4+ 10.Kf1 0-0 11.g4 According to Collijn, White has a strong attack.;

b) 7...Ba6! is much stronger, as if the bishop retreats to b3, then White can neither castle nor make use of f1. 8.Bxa6 Nxa6 9.Qe2 Nc5 10.0-0 Ne6 and White is running out of compensation for his pawn.

6.Qe2 Bb4+ 7.Nc3 b5!? 8.Bxb5 c6 9.Bc4 Qe7 with the idea of Bb7, 0-0, d5.

6.f4 d5!? was seen in a game V. Nielsen–P.Moeller, cited by Lutes.

6...	b6
7.0-0	Nc6
8.Ng3	Bb7
9.Nf5?!	Qg5!
10.h4	Qg6
11.h5	Qg5
12.f4	

12...	Bc5+!
13.Kh1	Qd8
14.Re1	Ne5!
15.Bxe5	

15.fxe5? Nxf5 with the threat of Qh4 mate.

15...	Nxf5
16.Qg4	

16.exf5?? Qh4+#

16...	Nh6
17.Qg3	

17.Qxg7?? Qh4+#

17...	Rg8

Now White remains on the defensive on the kingside.

18.Nc3 g6 19.Nd5 gxh5 20.Qh3 Ng4 21.Qxh5 Rg6 22.Ne3 Bxe3 23.Bxf7+

23.Rxe3 Nxe3 24.Bxf7+ Kxf7 25.f5 Qg5 26.fxg6+ Qxg6 27.Qf3+ Nf5! 28.Qxf5+ (28.exf5 Qh6+ 29.Qh3 Qxh3+-+) Qxf5 29.exf5 Rg8 30.Rg1 d6 with the idea of Rg5 -+.

23...Kxf7 24.f5 Qg5 25.fxg6+ Qxg6 26.Qf5+ Ke7 0-1.

Goldsmith–Handoko
Adelaide, 1990

1.e4 e5 2.d4 exd4 3.Qxd4

The old center game has fallen into complete disrepute. It is simply too slow.

3...   **Nc6**
4.Qe3

4.Qa4 Nf6 5.Bg5 (5.Nf3 d5! 6.Nc3 dxe4 7.Nxe4 Nxe4 8.Qxe4+ Qe7 9.Bd3 was seen in Sokotov–Michatek, correspondence 1968–70 and now instead of trading queens immediately, 9...Bf5 brings total equality, a point overlooked by Thinker's press in their 1990 article.) 5...Be7 6.Nc3 0-0 7.Nf3 d6 8.0-0-0 Bd7 9.Qc4 Be6 =. Milev–Chipev, Bulgarian Championhip 1961.

4...   **Nf6**
5.Nc3

5.e5 Ng4 6.Qe4 d5 7.exd6+ Be6 8.Ba6!? Qxd6 9.Bxb7 Qb4+ 10.Qxb4 Nxb4 =. was the interesting continuation of Mieses–Burn, Wroclaw 1912.

5...   **Bb4**
6.Bd2   **0-0**
7.0-0-0   **Re8**
8.Bc4   **Ne5!?**

8...d6 9.f3 Ne5 10.Bb3 Be6 =. Spielmann–Eliskases, Semmering 1937.

9.Bb3   **d6**
10.Nf3

10.f3 would transpose into the previous note.

10...   **Be6**
11.Bxe6   **Rxe6**
12.Nd4   **Re8**

12...Nc4? 13.Nxe6 Nxe3 14.Nxd8 Nxd1 15.Rxd1 Rxd8 16.f3 =.

13.Nf5   **Nc4**

White is now faced with tremendous pressure at e4, since the main defender, the knight at c3, is under attack.

14.Qg5	g6
15.Be1	Bxc3
16.Bxc3	Nxe4
17.Qh6	

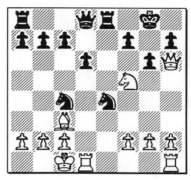

17...	Qg5+
18.Qxg5	Nxg5
19.Nh6+	Kf8
20.h4	

White must put all his energy into the attack, since otherwise he is a pawn down for nothing.

20...	Ne4

But the Black knights are too active!

21.Bh8

21.Bd4 c5 22.Be3 Nxe3 23.fxe3 Nf2?? (23...f5! ∓) 24.Rhf1 Nxd1 25.Rxf7+#.

21...	Nxf2
22.Rhf1	Re2
23.Bd4	

23.Rde1 Rae8 24.Rxe2 Rxe2 25.b3 Ne3.

23...Nxd1 24.Rxf7+ Ke8 25.Kxd1 Rd2+ 0-1.

Roscher–Andrae
Correspondence, 1989

1.e4 e5 2.c3

This is a slow attempt to occupy the center, and by reacting vigorously Black solves all of his opening problems.

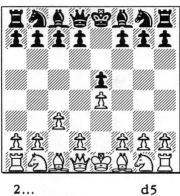

2...	d5
3.Qh5?!	

An unprincipled activation of the queen early in the game. But the alternatives do not pose any problems for Black either.

3.Nf3 Nc6 transposes to 2.Nf3 Nc6 3.c3, the Ponziani.

3.exd5 Qxd5 4.d4 Nc6 5.Be3 Bf5 6.Nf3 0-0-0 gives Black a good game.

3...	Bd6
4.exd5	Nf6
5.Qg5	

5.Qf3 Bg4 6.Qd3 e4 7.Qb5+ Nbd7 8.Qxb7 0-0 gives Black more than enough compensation for the pawn. Notice that Black has 4 pieces developed and has castled, while the only White piece in the game is the queen.

5...	0-0
6.Bc4	

White is wasting his time defending this pawn, but otherwise he is simply way behind in development.

6...	h6
7.Qh4	Bd7

7...Nbd7 with the idea of Nb6 is a worthwhile alternative.

8.Nf3	c6
9.dxc6	Nxc6
10.0-0	Bg4!

The threat of the capture at f3 keeps the pressure on.

11.Qg3	Be6!?
12.Ne1??	

At this point the game descends into gibberish. It is hard to believe that in a correspondence game neither player seems to have noticed that the bishop is hanging!

12.Bxe6 fxe6 leaves Black with doubled pawns but with a useful attacking file and threats of e5–e4.

12...	**Na5?**

12...Bxc4 13.d3 e4!

13.Qd3	**e4?**
14.Qd4	**Qc7**
15.Na3	**Bxh2+**
16Kh1	**Be5**

One wonders how such games get disseminated. It is clearly a result of the proliferation of computer databases. Although the end of the game was silly, I do think that the opening play was instructive. 0-1.

Dmitriyev–Rodin
Moscow, 1991

1.e4 e5 2.Bb5 Bc5 3.d3 Nc6 4.Nf3 Nge7 5.Be3 Bb6 6.Nbd2 0-0 7.Nc4 d6 8.Nxb6 axb6 9.d4 exd4 10.Nxd4 d5 11.Nxc6 bxc6 12.Bd3 dxe4 13.Bxe4 Qxd1+ 14.Kxd1 Bf5 15.Bxf5 Nxf5 16.Bf4 Rfd8+ 17.Kc1 Nd4 18.Re1 Ne6 19.Bg3 c5 20.b3 b5 21.Kb2 b4 22.a4 bxa3+ 23.Rxa3 Rxa3 24.Kxa3 Kf8 25.Kb2 Rd7 26.Kc3 Ke7 27.Bh4+ Ke8 28.f3 Rd5 29.Bf2 Kd7 30.h4 h5 31.g3 Kc6 32.f4 g6 33.Ra1 Kb5 34.Be3 Ng7 35.Rg1 Nf5 36.Bf2 Nd6 37.Re1 f5 38.Re2 Ne4+ 39.Kb2 c4 40.Be1 Rd1 41.Re3 c5 42.bxc4+ Kxc4 43.Re2 Kd4 44.Kb3 c4+ 45.Kb4 Rb1+ 46.Ka5 c3 47.Ka6 Rb2 48.Ka7 Kc5 49.Bf2+ Kd5 50.Bb6 Kc6 51.Bd4 Rb7+ 52.Ka8 Rd7 53.Be5 Rd2 54.Re1 Rxc2 55.Ra1 Kb6 56.Ra7 Rg2 57.Bd4+ Kb5 58.Rc7 Rxg3 59.Kb8 Rh3 60.Be5 Rxh4 0-1.

Queen's Gambit Declined I

(1.d4 d5 2.c4 e6 3.Nc3)

Kozlov–Kruppa
USSR , 1988

1.d4 d5 2.c4 e6 3.Nc3 Be7

We will be using this move order, an old idea of Alapin made popular by the Soviet player Alatortsev, to enter lines of the Queen's Gambit Declined that are somewhat off the beaten track, but which are solid and fully playable.

4.cxd5

4.e4 is an obvious move which might well be seen in amateur play, but which is not played at higher levels because Black can obtain an equal position without any difficulty. 4...dxe4 5.Nxe4 Nf6 Now White should just retreat the knight, as otherwise he gets into trouble. 6.Nxf6+? (6.Bd3 Qxd4 7.Nf3 Bb4+) Bxf6 7.Nf3 Nc6! and Black already has significant pressure, e.g., 8.Be3 0-0 9.Qd2 e5! 10.d5 Nd4 with a strong initiative for Black in Karasev–Tjulin, USSR 1968.

4...   exd5
5.Bf4

5.f3 was played by Andruet against Dutreeuw, Haringey 1988. It is an interesting idea, especially if one cooperates, as Black did, with 5...Nf6 6.e4 dxe4 7.fxe4. But it seems to me that the simple 5...Nc6!, placing indirect pressure at d4, is a much more sensible approach. White's position then looks artificial. Of course this option is not even mentioned by Thinker's Press (Tucker? Long?) in their 1990 article, which will perhaps have been the inspiration for your opponent's play. It is entirely possible that after 5...Nc6! the may want their money back!

5...   Nf6

This illustrates the point behind Black's move order. The bishop has been placed at f4, so now the knight can come out of hiding as if White chooses to annoy it by Bg5 it will have cost an extra tempo to do so.

6.e3	**0-0**
7.Bd3	**c5**
8.Nf3	

8.dxc5 Bxc5 9.Nge2 (9.Nf3 transposes below.) Nc6 10.0-0 d4! 11.exd4 Nxd4 12.Na4 Nxe2+ 13.Bxe2 Nd5! 14.Bg3 Be7 15.Qb3 Qa5 =. Anastasian–Kruppa, Minsk 1990.

8...	**Nc6**
9.0-0	

9.dxc5 Bxc5 10.0-0 d4 was seen in Murshed–Maric, Palma de Mallorca 1989, which quickly entered murky waters. 11.Ne4 (11.exd4 Nxd4 12.Nxd4 Qxd4 13.Be3 Qe5 14.Bxc5 Qxc5 15.Rc1 Qb6 16.Na4 Qa5 17.Rc5 Qd8 18.Be2 Qxd1 19.Rxd1 Bd7 20.Nc3 Bc6 =. was seen in Vyzhmanavin–Kuzmin, Moscow 1986. Although White managed to chase the enemy queen for some time, this position holds no advantage for him. Or 11.Na4 Bd6 12.Bxd6 Qxd6 13.Nxd4 Nxd4 14.exd4 Bg4! =.) dxe3 12.Qe2 exf2+ 13.Kh1 and now instead of 13...Qb6, there was a more secure path with 13... Nd4 14.Nxf6+ Qxf6 15.Qe4? Bf5 16.Qe5 Bxd3 17.Qxc5 (17.Qxf6 gxf6 18.Nxd4 Bxd4 19.Rfd1 f1Q+) Bxf1 18.Qxd4 Qxd4 19.Nxd4 Bd3-+

9...	**c4**

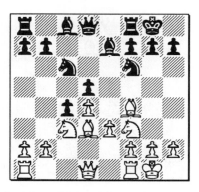

An important decision. This reduces pressure in the center and allows White to prepare counterplay with e3–e4, but at the same time it makes it more difficult for White to expose the weakness of the pawn at d5.

10.Be2

10.Bc2 Bg4 (10…Nh5?! 11.Be5 f6 12.Ng5! g6 13.Nxh7 fxe5 14.Nxf8 Bxf8 15.dxe5 Be6 16.Bxg6 Ng7 17.f4 gave White a strong attack in Olafsson–Einarsson, Reykjavik 1988.) 11.h3 Bh5 and the bishop will contest the light squares from g6.

10…	Nh5

11.Be5

A provocative move. Here the exchange of minor pieces would only help White, but Black wisely chooses another path.

11…	f6!

This would seem to weaken the light squares and limit the scope of the bishop at e7 but in fact it plays an important defensive role, controlling e5.

12.Bg3	Nxg3
13.hxg3	Be6
14.Qc2	Rc8
15.Rad1	Bb4!

This applies pressure at c3 so that White's control of e4 is reduced.

16.e4

White has little choice but to play in the center, but the Tarrasch pawn structure is very solid since there is no pressure on the a8–h1 diagonal as is usual in Tarrasch games.

16…	Ne7

17.e5

17.exd5 Nxd5 18.Nxd5 Bxd5 19.Qa4 Qa5 ∓

17…	Nc6

18.a3

18.Rfe1!? fxe5 19.Nxe5 (19.dxe5 d4) Nxe5 20.dxe5 Qg5!? is messy, but I think that Black has the better prospects.

18...	Ba5
19.Qd2	

White's last two moves have created significant weaknesses which can be exploited once the central situation is clarified.

19...	fxe5
20.Nxe5	Nxe5
21.dxe5	Qe8!

The pin at c3 is annoying so White wastes a move to break it.

22.Qc1	Rd8
23.Bf3	d4
24.Ne4	d3

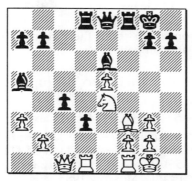

The cramping effect of the Black pawns is obvious.

25.Nc5	b5
26.Nb7	

White's position is so bad that he must accept the offer of the exchange, but the knight was the only active piece in his arsenal.

26.Nxe6 Qxe6 27.Qe3 Bb6 would be most unpleasant for White.

26...	Bb6
27.Nxd8	Qxd8
28.Bc6	a6
29.a4	bxa4!
30.Bxa4	Qd4

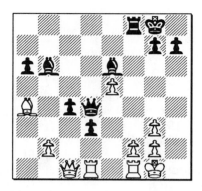

Each bishop is now more powerful than either of the White rooks.

31.Qd2	Bd5
32.Qe1	Bb7
33.Kh2	

White must do something about the threat of Qd5. 33… Rf5 34.g4 Qxg4 But there was another path to g2. 0-1.

Timoshchenko,V–Kruppa
Frunze, 1988

1.d4 d5 2.c4 e6 3.Nc3 Be7 4.cxd5 exd5 5.Bf4 Nf6 6.e3

6.Qc2 0-0 7.e3 c5! 8.dxc5 Bxc5 9.Nf3 Nc6 10.Be2 (10.Bb5? d4 11.Bxc6 dxc3 12.Qxc3 Qe7! 13.Ba4 Bb4-+) d4! 11.exd4 (11.0-0-0 Nb4 12.Qb1 Nbd5! 13.Nxd5 Qxd5 14.Nxd4 =.) Nxd4 12.Nxd4 Qxd4 =. Karpov–Kasparov, 20th match game, Moscow 1985.

6…   0-0

Now White must determine how to develop his pieces. 7.Bd3 is the most common move, but in this game we examine the alternatives.

7.Nf3

7.Qc2 is interesting, and led to a rare defeat by Anatoly Karpov during his reign as World Champion. 7...c6 8.Bd3 Re8 9.Nf3 Nbd7 This knight will soon get out of the way and allow the bishop at c8 to be developed. 10.0-0-0 White castles queenside, a wise move since Black is swinging his forces to the kingside. 10...Nf8 11.h3 Be6 (11...Bb4 12.Kb1 Qe7 13.Bg5 Qe6 is Karpov's suggestion, with the clear positional point of contesting the e4- square.) 12.Kb1 Rc8 13.Ng5 In Timman–Karpov, Bugojno 1978, the world champion made the decisive error of launching his attack by advancing the b-pawn, and lost. But he provides a better plan in his notes to the game. 13...c5! 14.dxc5 Bxc5 and here the fact that the Ng5 cannot operate on d4 works to Black's advantage according to Karpov.

7...	Bf5

8.Qb3

8.Ne5 c5 9.g4 looks aggressive but Black need not worry. 9...cxd4 10.exd4 Be6 11.Bg2 Nc6 12.h3 was seen in Dohosian–Kruppa, Sevastopol 1986, but here Black can equalize with 12...Qb6!

8.h3 c6 9.g4 Bg6 10.Ne5 Nfd7! 11.Nxg6 fxg6 12.Bg2 (12.Bd3 Nb6 13.Qe2 c5 would give Black counterplay, according to Karpov.) Nb6 13.0-0 Kh8 14.Ne2 g5 15.Bg3 Bd6 =. Karpov–Kasparov, 22nd match game, Moscow 1985.

8...	Nc6
9.a3!?	Na5
10.Qa2	Be6!?

The idea here is to reinforce the light squares on the queenside so that c4 can be used. It also contains the idea that after ...Ne4, a capture by White will result in an attack on his own queen.

11.Be2

11.b4 Nc4! 12.Bxc4 dxc4 13.e4 gives White control of the center, but Black can obtain immediate counterplay. 13...a5! 14.d5 Bg4 15.Qxc4 axb4 16.Nb5 c6 17.dxc6 bxc6 18.Qxc6 Bxf3 19.gxf3 Qd3! ∓

11...	c5
12.Rd1	Ne4!

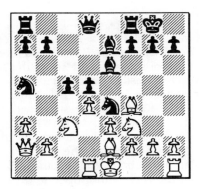

This well timed thrust eliminates any chance of an advantage for White, who must now struggle merely to maintain the balance.

13.Nxe4

13.0-0 Nxc3 14.bxc3 Rc8 Black has pressure building on the c-file and in the endgame the White a-pawn is a weakness. White has no compensatory positional factors, so Black stands better .

13...	dxe4
14.d5	Bg4

14...Bf5!? is suggested in Informant.

15.Nd2!?

15.Nd4!? Bxe2 16.Nxe2 Bd6 17.0-0 Bxf4 18.Nxf4 Qd6 is, in my opinion, not unclear, as stated in Informant, but rather better for Black, whose blockade is secure and who enjoys a free hand on the queenside. I just don't see where White is going with his position.

15...	Bxe2
16.Kxe2	Qd7
17.h3	

17.Nxe4!? Qg4+ 18.f3 Qxg2+ 19.Nf2 Qg6 looks to be better for Black. Informant gives the following analysis: 20.Qb1 (20.d6 Bf6 21.Ne4 Qg2+ 22.Nf2 Qg6 23.Ne4 ∞.) Qa6+ 21.Qd3 c4! 22.Qc3 Bf6 23.Be5 Bxe5 24.Qxe5 c3+ 25.Rd3 ∓

17...	Qb5+

17...Qa4!? also comes into consideration, keeping the pressure on the light squares on the queenside.

18.Ke1	Bf6
19.Nxe4	Bxb2

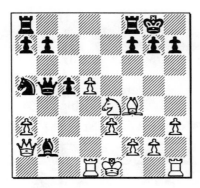

20.Rd2!?

20.Rb1 Qd3 21.Qxb2 Qxe4 22.Bc7 Nc4 23.Qxb7 Nxa3 with the idea of Nc2+ and Black is clearly in command. (23...Qxg2 24.d6!).

20...	Nc4?

Black misses the critical move here, as pointed out in Informant.

20...Qa4! 21.Rxb2! (21.Nxc5 Qxa3 22.Qxa3 Bxa3 23.Bd6!? Rfd8 24.Bc7 Bxc5 25.Bxa5 b6 26.Bc3 a5 ∓) Qxe4 22.f3 Qf5 (22...Qd3 23.Rd2) 23.Kf2 Rac8 ∓

21.Rc2	Ne5
22.Nxc5	Rfc8
23.Qxb2	Rxc5
24.Bxe5!	

Now White has turned the tables.

24...	Qxb2
25.Rxb2	Rc1+
26.Ke2	Rxh1
27.Rxb7	

Despite the extra exchange Black is hopelessly lost, because of the combined power of the pawn and bishop.

27...	Rc1
28.d6?	

White returns the favor, and allows Black back into the game.

28.Bc7! was the right move, so that the bishop covers both d6 and d8, for example: Kf8 29.d6 Ke8 30.Ba5 Rc2+ 31.Kd3+-

28...f	6!
29.Bd4?	

The win was still there:

29.Bg3 a5 30.d7 Rc2+ (30...Rd8 31.Rb8+-) 31.Kd3 Rc1 32.Kd2 Rc5 33.e4 Rc4 34.Ke3 Rc1 35.e5 fxe5 36.Bxe5 Rc5 37.Kd4 Rc1 38.Kd5 Rd1+ 39.Bd4 Rd8

	29...	Rd8!

30.Rxa7 Rxd6 31.a4 Rc2+! 32.Kf3 Ra2 33.a5 Rd5! 34.a6 Rf5+ 35.Ke4 Rfxf2 36.Ra8+ Kf7 37.a7 Ra5 38.Rh8 Rfa2 39.Rxh7? Kg8! 40.Rh4 R2a4! 41.Kf3 Rxa7 1/2–1/2

Fayard–Spassky
French Championship, 1991
1.d4 d5 2.c4 e6 3.Nc3 Be7 4.Nf3

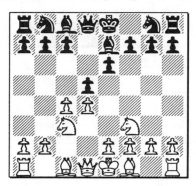

White often chooses this less aggressive plan, hoping to transpose into more usual lines.

	4...	Nf6
	5.Bg5	h6
	6.Bxf6	

In this game we examine the lines where White captures immediately.

	6...	Bxf6
	7.e3	

This is a timid move which allows Black to obtain a comfortable game without difficulty.

	7...	0-0
	8.Qd2	c6
	9.0-0-0	

White goes for broke. Normal kingside development would not do anything to justify White's parting with the bishop pair.

	9...	Nd7
	10.e4?!	

This just weakens the center.

	10...	dxc4
	11.Bxc4	c5!

12.e5

12.d5 Nb6

12...	cxd4
13.Qxd4	

13.exf6 dxc3 14.Qxc3 Qxf6 ∓

13...	Be7
14.Qe4	Qa5

The central situation has been resolved. White has control of the territory but his pawn at e5 requires support and his king is now vulnerable.

15.Bd3	g6
16.Qf4	

If only White still had a dark-squared bishop!

16...	Kg7
17.h4	Nc5
18.Bc2	

18.Bb1 would have left the king without room to maneuver.

18...	Bd7
19.Nh2	

19.h5 g5 20.Qg4 f5 21.exf6+ Bxf6 and Black's attack is faster, e.g., 22.Rxd7+ Nxd7 23.Qxe6 Rf7 24.Qe4 Bxc3 25.Qg6+ Kf8 26.bxc3 (26.Qxh6+ Bg7 27.Qxg5 Qxg5+ 28.Nxg5 Rxf2 29.h6 Bh8 and White has nothing to show for the rook.) Qxc3 27.Qxh6+ Kg8 28.Qg6+ Qg7 and Whtie is just a rook down.

19...	Bc6
20.Ng4	Rh8
21.Nf6	

Although White seems to have an attack, the queen and knight do not accomplish much, and the rook provides more than enough defense.

21...	Rad8
22.Rxd8	Rxd8
23.h5	g5
24.Qe3	Qb4!

Preventing f2–f4, after which White might be able to crack open the kingside.

25.Rf1	Qd4
26.Qg3	

26.Qxd4 Rxd4 and Black has all the play.

26...	Nd3+!
27.Bxd3	Qxd3
28.Qxd3	Rxd3

29.Kc2   Rd4

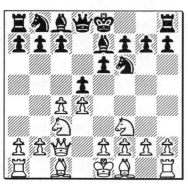

White suffers from "Caro-Kann pawns" on the kingside, and also is playing with knights against bishops where the latter have more scope.

30.Ne2	Rd8
31.f3	Bxf6!
32.exf6+	Kxf6
33.Kc3	Bb5

Now it is just technique.

34.Re1 Rd3+ 35.Kb4 Bc6 36.Nc3 Rd2 0-1.

Cosma–Geller
Berlin, 1991

1.d4 d5 2.c4 e6 3.Nc3 Be7 4.Nf3 Nf6 5.Qc2

A conservative plan.

5...	0-0
6.cxd5	exd5

7.Bf4	c5!
8.dxc5	

8.e3 Nc6 and the queen certainly looks misplaced at c2.

8...	Nc6
9.e3	Bxc5
10.a3	

White has no pressure against Black's isolated pawn, and insufficient control of the d-file. So Black can eliminate his problem pawn and take over the initiative.

10...	d4
11.0-0-0	

11.exd4 Nxd4 12.Nxd4 Qxd4 (12...Bxd4 =.) 13.Be3 Re8 14.Be2 Rxe3!? 15.fxe3 Qxe3 16.Rf1 Bg4 might be worth the investment of an exchange for a pawn.

11...	Bg4
12.Be2	Rc8!

Despite the presence of many pieces on the c-file, this move creates major threats.

13.Kb1	Qa5
14.Nb5	

14.exd4 Bxf3 15.dxc5 (15.Bxf3 Nxd4 16.Qd3 Nxf3 17.Qxf3 Bxa3!) Bxe2 16.Nxe2 b6 17.Bd6 Rfd8 ∞.

14...	Be7
15.Nd6	Bxd6
16.Bxd6	Rfd8

White's maneuver has not improved his position. Now the Black forces are well prepared for battle.

17.Qc5	Qxc5
18.Bxc5	Ne4
19.Rc1	d3!

The failure to remove this pawn moved up White's execution date.

20.Bd1 d2 21.Rc4 Nxf2 22.Rf1 Bf5+ 0-1.

Queen's Gambit Declined II

(1.d4 d5 2.c4 e6 3.Nf3 Be7)

Karpov–Kasparov
Moscow (m/21), 1984

**1.Nf3 d5 2.d4 Nf6 3.c4 e6 4.Nc3 Be7 5.Bg5 h6 6.Bxf6 Bxf6
7.Qd2**

This move achieved prominence in the 1984/85 marathon World
Championship match .

7.e4 dxe4 8.Nxe4 Nc6!

a) 9.d5 Ne5 10.Nxf6+ (10.Be2 0-0 11.Qb3 exd5 12.cxd5 c6! and Black
was better in Romanishin–Geller, USSR Championship 1978. The White
king is very exposed.) Qxf6 11.Nxe5 Qxe5+ 12.Qe2 Qf6! 13.g3 0-0
14.Bg2 =. Nikolic–Tal, Wijk aan Zee 1982.;

b) 9.Nxf6+ Qxf6 10.Qd2 (10.Qd3 b6 11.Qe4 Bb7 12.Ne5 0-0-0!
13.Nxc6 Rd6 =. Tatai–Geller, Las Palmas 1979.) Bd7 =. 11.Qe3 0-0-0!
12.Be2 Rhe8 13.0-0 Kb8 14.Ne5 Nxe5 15.dxe5 Qg5 and a draw was
agreed in Vladimirov–Kholmov, Leningrad 1967.

7.Qb3 must be countered vigorously. 7...c5! With d4 deprived of the
support of the queen, this move places great pressure on the center.
8.dxc5 dxc4 9.Qxc4 0-0 Black does not have to hurry to regain his
pawn, since White is so far behind in his development. 10.Rc1 Bd7

a 11.e3?! Qe7! 12.Bd3 Bc6 13.e4 Nd7 14.b4 b6! 15.b5 (15.cxb6 Nxb6
16.Qxc6 Rac8 17.Qb5 Bxc3+ 18.Ke2 Qxb4) Bd5! and Black was better in
Malaniuk–Kruppa, USSR 1986, since 16.exd5? fails to 16...exd5+,
winning the queen;

b) 11.g3 Qa5 12.Bg2 Bb5! 13.Qb3 (13.Qxb5?? Bxc3+) Bc6 14.0-0 Na6
and in Lerner–Belyavsky, USSR Championship 1986, Black was ready to
reclaim his material and the chances were even.

| 7... | **dxc4!** |

With the bishop at f6, there is already enough pressure on d4 to
justify this move.

| **8.e4** | **c5** |

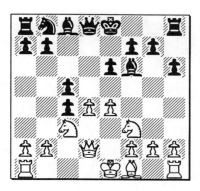

Black adopts a hypermodern strategy here, allowing White to build a big center only to bash away at it in the opening.

9.d5

9.e5 cxd4 10.exf6 dxc3 11.Qxd8+ Kxd8 12.fxg7 Rg8 13.Bxc4 Rxg7 with a good game for Black, according to Mikhalchischin.

| **9..** | **exd5** |
| **10.e5** | |

10.Nxd5 Nc6 11.Nxf6+ Qxf6 12.Bxc4 0-0 is fine for Black.

| **10...** | **Bg5!** |
| **11.Qxd5** | |

11.Nxg5 hxg5 12.Nxd5 Rh4! with the idea of Rd4.

| **11...** | **Nc6** |
| **12.Bxc4** | |

12.Qxc5 Be6 13.Bxc4 Be7! 14.Qb5 a6 15.Qxb7 Na5 ∓

| **12...** | **0-0** |
| **13.0-0** | |

13.Qxc5 Bg4 gives Black a strong initiative.

13.Qe4 Re8 and the e-file is a danger zone for White.

| **13...** | **Qxd5** |
| **14.Bxd5** | |

14.Nxd5 Be6 15.Nc7 Bxc4 16.Nxa8 Bxf1 17.Kxf1 Rxa8-+

| **14...** | **Nb4!** |

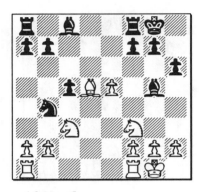

15.Nxg5

15.Bc4 Bf5 and the light squares are extremely vulnerable.

15.Be4 f5! 16.Bd5+ (16.exf6 Bxf6 ∓ or 16.Bb1 Be6 and Black has a much better position.) Nxd5 17.Nxd5 Bd8! and in Ubilava–Dorfman, USSR Championship Prelims 1984, Black's bishop pair was strong enough to offset the advanced pawn. The game concluded in a draw after Black exchanged both bishops for the knights. 18.Rfd1 Re8 19.Rac1 b6 20.b4 cxb4 21.Nxb4 Bb7 22.Nc6 (22.Rd7 Bxf3 23.gxf3 Rxe5) Bg5! 23.Nxg5 hxg5 24.Rd7 Bxc6 25.Rxc6 Rad8! and a draw was soon agreed.

15...	Nxd5
16.Nxd5	hxg5
17.f4!	

The only chance to play for the advantage. Indeed, if White is not careful the initiative will fall into Black's hands.

17.Rfd1 Be6 18.Nc7 Rad8 19.Nxe6 fxe6 20.Kf1 Kf7 and the weakness of the e-pawn combined with the queenside majority give Black an advantage.

17...	gxf4
18.Rxf4	

18.Ne7+ Kh7 19.Rxf4 gives White an attack, but it is not a very strong one. 19...g6 20.Rc1 (20.Rf6?! Kg7 21.Raf1 Bd7 22.e6 Bxe6 23.Nxg6 Rfe8! 24.Nh4 Bxa2) b6 21.b4 Be6! 22.bxc5 Rfe8 23.Nc6 bxc5 24.Rxc5 Bxa2 25.Ra5 Rac8 26.Nxa7 (26.Rxa2 Rxc6 27.Rxa7 Rc1+ 28.Kf2 Rc2+ and the game should be drawn.) Rc1+ 27.Rf1 Rxf1+ 28.Kxf1 Bc4+ 29.Kf2 g5 and Black should be able to hold the endgame.

18...	Rd8!
19.Nc7	Rb8
20.Raf1	Rd7

Though Black's position is a bit grovelly, he isn't in any real danger.

21.Nb5	Re7
22.Nxa7	Bd7
23.a4	

Necessary, in order to extract the knight.

23...	Ra8
24.Nb5	Bxb5

24..g5 25.Re4 would have been messier.

25.axb5	Ra5
26.b6	Rb5

At this point the press thought that a draw was likely, but Karpov gave it one more push.

27.b4!

27...	cxb4

27...Rxb4 28.Rxb4 cxb4 29.Re1 f6 30.e6 b3 31.Kf2 b2 32.Kf3 b1Q 33.Rxb1 Rxe6 =.

28.Rb1	b3
29.Rf3	b2
30.Rf2	Rexe5!

30...Rxb6 31.Rfxb2 Rxb2 32.Rxb2 Kf8 33.Kf2 Rxe5 34.Rxb7

31.Rfxb2

And a draw was agreed. 1/2–1/2.

Karpov–Kasparov
Moscow (m/23), 1984

1.Nf3 d5 2.d4 Nf6 3.c4 e6 4.Nc3 Be7 5.Bg5 h6 6.Bh4 0-0
7.Rc1

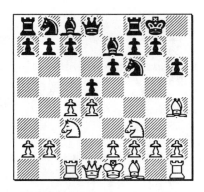

White adopts an old classical approach to the opening, with the twist that he has developed his knight rather than playing e2–e3.

7...   dxc4!?

This invites White to play e2–e4, but we will see in another game that there is nothing to be gained by building a big center, since Black can tear it down quickly. Karpov chooses the quieter path.

8.e3

8.e4 Nc6 9.e5 (9.Bxc4 Nxe4 10.Bxe7 Nxc3 11.Bxd8 Nxd1 12.Bxc7 Nxb2 13.Bb5 a6 14.Bxc6 Nd3+ 15.Kd2 Nxc1 16.Be4 Nxa2 17.Bd6 Rd8 18.Bc5 e5 19.Nxe5 Nb4 is the marvelous forcing line given by Belyavsky.) Nd5 10.Bxe7 Ncxe7 11.Bxc4 Nxc3 12.bxc3 b6 13.Qe2 Bb7 14.Ba6 Bd5! 15.0-0 c5 16.dxc5 bxc5 17.Bc4 Bc6! 18.Bb5 =. Tukmakov–Biyavsky, Tilburg 1984. As long as Black preserves his light-squared bishop he has nothing to worry about.

8...   c5!

9.Bxc4

9.dxc5 Qxd1+ 10.Kxd1 Rd8+ 11.Kc2 Bxc5 =. Agdestein–Andersson, Naestved 1985.

9...   cxd4

10.Nxd4

10.exd4 Nc6 11.0-0 Nh5! 12.Bxe7 Nxe7 13.Bb3 (13.Re1 Nf6 14.Ne5 Bd7 15.Qb3 Rb8 16.Rcd1 b5! 17.Nxd7 Nxd7 18.Bd3 Nf6 19.Bb1 a6 20.Ne4 Ned5 =. Christiansen–Karpov, London 1982.)(13.d5 exd5 14.Nxd5 Nxd5 15.Qxd5 Qxd5 16.Bxd5 Nf4! brought Black equality in Uhlmann–Kurajica, Sarajevo 1982.) Nf6 14.Ne5 Bd7 15.Qe2 Rc8 =. Korchnoi–Karpov, (m/9) 1981.

10...   Bd7

11.0-0

11.Be2 Nc6 12.Nb3 Nd5! =. Korchnoi–Karpov, Merano (m/17) 1981.

11...   Nc6

12.Nb3	Rc8
13.Be2	

13...	Nd5!
14.Bxe7	

14.Bg3 Ncb4 gives Black the initiative.

14...Ncxe7 15.Nxd5 Nxd5 16.Rxc8 Qxc8 17.Qd4 Qb8! 18.Bf3 Nf6 19.Nc5 Bb5 20.Rd1 b6 21.Ne4 Nxe4 22.Bxe4 Rc8   1/2–1/2.

Ree–Hjartarson
Reykjavik, 1984

1.d4 Nf6 2.c4 e6 3.Nf3 d5 4.Bg5 Be7 5.Nc3 h6 6.Bh4 0-0 7.Qc2

7.Qb3 c5 8.dxc5 Nbd7 9.e3 Nxc5 10.Qc2 b6 11.Rd1 Bb7 12.Be2 Nfe4 =. Kurajica–Kir.Georgiev, Sarajevo 1985.

7...	b6

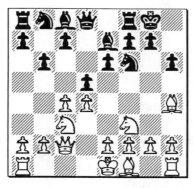

The e4-square is going to play an important role in this line, so Black plans to use the long diagonal. White reacts by eliminating the Nf6.

8.Bxf6

8.Rd1 Bb7 9.Bxf6 Bxf6 10.cxd5 exd5 11.g3 Qe7 12.Bg2 Rd8 13.0-0 Na6 14.Ne1 c5 15.dxc5 Bxc3 16.c6 Bxc6 =. Petrosian–Klovans, Jurmala 1983.

8.e3 c5!? 8...Bb7 would transpose to the Main Lines of the Tartakower Variation, but there is no need to learn all that theory, because this move is even better. 9.dxc5 (9.cxd5 Nxd5 10.Bxe7 Qxe7 11.Nxd5 exd5 12.dxc5 bxc5 13.Rc1 Na6 14.Qa4 Qf6! 15.Bb5 Rb8 16.0-0 Rb6 =. Kotov–Bondarevsky, USSR Championship 1939.) bxc5 10.Rd1 Qa5 11.Be2 (11.Bxf6?! Bxf6 12.cxd5 exd5 13.Rxd5 Nc6 14.Rd2 Rb8 15.Nd5 Bxb2 and White's game is a mess—analysis in ECOII (1987).) Nbd7! 12.0-0 Bb7 and here ECOII (1987) evaluates the position as unclear. Karpov was the person responsible for this section, and he understands the hanging pawn structure very well. Black's forces are well-coordinated.

8...	Bxf6
9.e4	

The opening has followed a logical course. The pawn at d4 is taboo because of the recapture with the queen. Black had previously countered with c7–c5, but there is an even more aggressive reply.

9...	Nc6!
10.0-0-0	

A reasonable method of defending the d-pawn, though there were, of course, other options.

10.e5 Be7 11.cxd5 Nb4 12.Qb3 Nxd5 13.Nxd5 exd5 and Black stands better, according to Hjartarson, because the bishop pair will be strong.

10.Rd1 dxe4 11.Qxe4 Bb7 12.Bd3 g6 13.0-0 Bg7 =.—Hjartarson.

10...	dxe4
11.Qxe4	Bb7
12.Bd3	g6
13.h4	

If White castles queenside in the Queen's Gambit, a kingside pawnstorm is usually what he has in mind.

13...	Rb8
14.Qg4	Bg7
15.Be2	

The d-pawn requires defense.

15...	Ne7!
16.h5	

16.Ne5 h5 with the idea of Qd6.

16...	g5
17.Ne5	Nf5
18.Bf3	

Black's kingside is well defended. Now comes a surprising break in the center.

18...	c5!
19.dxc5	Qc7
20.Nd7	Bxc3!
21.bxc3?	

21.cxb6 was the only move. Hjartarson gives the following analysis: Bxb2+ 22.Kxb2 Bxf3 23.Qxf3 Nd6 24.Nxb8 Nxc4+ 25.Kc2 Nxb6+ 26.Nc6 Nd5 27.Kb2 Qxc6 28.Ka1 Qc5 and here claims that Black has sufficient compensation. I think that Black actually has a clear advantage here, as the White pawns will be vulnerable in any endgame.

21...	bxc5
22.Nxf8	Qa5!
23.Kd2	

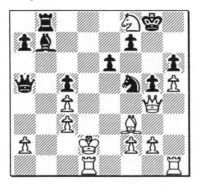

23...	Nd4!
24.Ke1	Nxf3+
25.Kf1	

25.gxf3 Qxc3+ 26.Kf1 Bxf3 27.Qg3 Qd3+!!-+

25...Qa4! 26.Rd6 f5 0-1.

Queen's Gambit Declined III

(1.d4 d5 2.c4 e6 3.Nf3 Nf6)

We have been suggesting that Black play 3...Be7. But in our repertoire we must also be concerned with alternative move orders, such as 1.c4 e6 2.Nf3 d5 3.cxd5 exd5 4.d4 and in the confusion of the multiple move orders it is easy for Black to play an early Nf6. So here are a couple of examples of the Queen's Gambit where White plays an early Nf3, and Black has developed his knight. This is also an area where Black can afford to add a little variety to the repertoire.

Simagin–Tal
Kislovodsk, 1966

1.d4 Nf6 2.c4 e6 3.Nf3 d5 4.cxd5 exd5 5.Nc3

White plans to steer the game into the Exchange Variation, but Black has an interesting option.

5.Qc2 Bb4+ 6.Bd2 Nc6 7.a3 Bxd2+ 8.Nbxd2 Ne7! and the threat of Bf5 brought Black equality in Tarasov–Antoshin, USSR Ch 1957 .

5...　　　　　　　　Ne4!?

This move violates the principle about moving pieces twice in the opening, but the knight occupies an important square and eliminates any chance of Bg5.

6.Qb3

6.Bf4 is suggested by V.Sokolov in Informant 2. ECO II (1987) evaluates it as a bit better for White, but I am not sure why. 6...Nxc3 7.bxc3 c5 and I doubt White can take the pawn. 8.Bxb8 Rxb8 9.Qa4+

Bd7 10.Qxa7 Ra8 11.Qxb7 cxd4 12.Nxd4 (12.cxd4 Qa5+ 13.Nd2 Bb4
14.Rd1 Ke7 with the idea of Rhb8.) Qa5 13.Kd2 (13.Rc1 Qxa2 ∓) Rc8
14.Qb2 Bd6 and Black has the bishop pair, a safer king and an initiative
for the pawn.

6.g3 is also suggested by V.Sokolov, but the same plan is even more
effective here. 6… Nxc3 7.bxc3 c5 8.Bg2 Nc6 9.0-0 cxd4 10.cxd4 Be7
and Black has a fine Tarrasch formation.

6…	c6
7.Bf4	Bd6
8.Bxd6	Nxd6!

Black has a solid position and equality is not far away.

9.e3	Bf5
10.Be2	Nd7
11.0-0	0-0
12.Rfe1	Re8

13.Nd2?!
13.Qa3! would have kept the playing field level.

13…	Re6
14.Nf1	Qh4

Black has already whipped up a strong attack.

15.g3	Qg5
16.Bf3	Nf6
17.Bg2	Rae8

White has improved his defenses but Black has used this time to get
his pieces in optimal position.

18.f3?!
18.Nd2 would have been best, according to V.Sokolov.

18…	Bd3?

Tal returns the favor.

18...Qg6! would have given Black complete domination of the light-squares.

19.Nxd5!	Nxd5
20.Qxd3	Nxe3
21.Bh3!	R6e7
22.f4	

A critical moment. Should the queens come off?

22...	Qg6?!

22...Qh5! 23.Bg2 Nxg2 24.Rxe7 Rxe7 25.Kxg2 Qe2+ 26.Qxe2 Rxe2+ 27.Kf3 Rxb2 and Black should win the endgame.

23.Qxg6	hxg6
24.Rac1	Nd5
25.Rxe7	Rxe7

Despite Black's active pieces, there are no real winning chances here.

26.Bg2	Nf5
27.Bxd5	cxd5
28.Kf2	f6
29.Rc5	1/2–1/2.

Grunberg–Petursson
Moscow, 1989

1.d4 Nf6 2.c4 e6 3.Nf3 d5 4.Bg5 dxc4

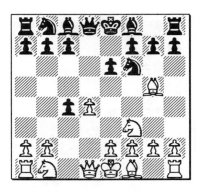

This position resembles a Queen's Gambit Accepted, but with a very early deployment of White's dark-squared bishop

5.Qa4+

5.Nc3 a6 6.e4 b5 This position is similar to those of the Semi-slav, with the very important difference that the c-pawn is still on its home square, and can go to c5 without loss of time, as we shall see. 7.e5 h6 8.Bh4 g5 9.Nxg5 A typical sacrifice in these structures. The pin at f6 will guarantee the return of the material. 9...hxg5 10.Bxg5 Nbd7 11.Be2 c5! and here ECO II notes that Black had compensation in Razuvayev−Sveshnikov, USSR Championship 1979.

5.e3 b5 6.a4 c6 7.Nc3 brings us back to the Semi-Slav, but here I like an untested idea by the theoretician Sveshnikov: 7...a6!? 8.axb5 cxb5 9.Nxb5 axb5! 10.Rxa8 Bb4+ with the idea of Bb7. Black has plenty of compensation here, with active pieces, an intiative on the queenside and a big lead in development in return for the exchange.

5...　　　　　　　　　　　Nbd7
6.Qxc4

White doesn't have to recapture the pawn immediately, but the alternatives are not promising.

6.g3 a6 7.Qxc4 b5 8.Qc1 Bb7 leads to a sort of Catalan formation. 9.Bg2 Rc8! but with the difference that Black's counterplay comes very quickly, as in Gheorghiu−Ribli, Lucerne 1985. White is already on the defensive.

6.e4 Be7 puts immediate pressure at e4. A) 7.e5 Nd5 8.Bxe7 Qxe7 9.Bxc4 Qb4+ 10.Qxb4 Nxb4 11.Bb3 c5! ∓ (11...Nd3+ 12.Kd2 Nxb2 13.Kc3 ±); B) 7.Nbd2 0 -0 8.Bxc4 c5! is Larsen's suggestion. Black has emerged from the opening with a good game.

6.e3 c5! 7 Bxc4 cxd4 8.exd4 Be7 9.Nc3 0-0 brought Black equality in Andersson−Ribli, Tilburg 1984.

6.Nbd2 Be7 7.Qxc4 0-0 8.e3 b6! 9.Be2 Bb7 10.0-0 c5 was agreed drawn in Portisch–Miles, Tilburg 1984. The delay in recapturing the pawn gives Black time to develop smoothly in all of these cases.

6...	**c5**
7.Nc3	

7.Nbd2 a6 8.dxc5 Bxc5 is not going to get White anything. 9.b4 b5! 10.Qb3 Be7 11.e4 Bb7 12.Bd3 h6 13.Be3 Ng4 14.Bd4 Nde5! =. Dolmatov–Sveshnikov, Manila 1982.

7...	**a6**
8.dxc5	

8.a4 b5! 9.axb5? axb5 ∓

8...	**Bxc5**
9.e3	**b5**
10.Qh4	**Bb7**

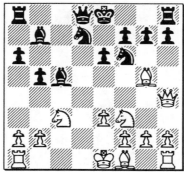

It is clear that Black has won the opening battle, with control of space in the center and on the queenside.

11.Be2	**b4!**
12.Na4	**Be7**

Now the knight is offside.

13.0-0	**Qa5**
14.b3	**h6**
15.Rac1	**0-0**
16.Bxf6	**Nxf6**
17.Nd2	

The knight on the rim can be made more useful if there is a companion steed at c4 which will support an invasion at b6. But Black gains time by nipping at the horse.

17...	**Rad8**
18.Nc4	**Qf5**
19.Qg3	

19.Nab6 Ne4 20.Qg4 Nc3! 21.Qxf5? Nxe2+ 22.Kh1 exf5

19...	Bd5
20.Bf3	

20.Nab6 Ne4 21.Qg4 Nc3 as above.

20...	Ne4
21.Bxe4	Bxe4
22.Nab6	

Finally! But now that the knight has arrived, the view is not so promising, since there are not many targets in the area. The bishop pair is powerful.

22...h5 23.Rfe1 h4 24.Qf4 Bf6

24...Qxf4 25.exf4 Bf5 26.Ne5 and White's command of space offsets the bishop pair.

25.Qxf5 exf5

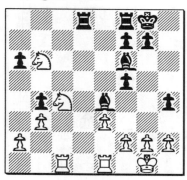

Black has accepted the pawn weakness, but gains some space and the bishops are firmly planted in attractive positions.

26.h3	Rd3
27.Red1	Rfd8
28.Rxd3	Rxd3
29.Na4	

A big concession, but the knight wasn't doing anything at b6.

29...	Be7
30.Kf1	Rd8
31.f3	

31.Ke2 g5 32.Nd2 Bd3+ 33.Ke1 Bf6 and White is paralyzed.

31...	Bc6
32.Ke2	g5
33.Nab2	g4
34.Nd3	

34.fxg4 Bxg2 35.gxf5 Bxh3 36.Rg1+ Kh7 37.e4 Rd4 38.Ke3 Bc5 ∓

34...	g3

This secures a long-term advantage in the endgame.

35.Nf4	Bb5
36.Nd3	a5!
37.Rd1	a4
38.Ndb2	Rxd1
39.Nxd1	

39.Kxd1 a3 40.Nd3 Bxc4 41.bxc4 b3 42.axb3 a2-+

39...	Bxc4+
40.bxc4	a3

Creating threats of b4–b3, as well as trapping the knight.

41.Kd3	Kg7
42.f4	

42.e4 f4!

42...	Kf6
43.Kc2	

43.e4 fxe4+ 44.Kxe4 b3

43...	Ke6
44.Kb3	Kd7
45.e4	

45Kc2 Kc6 46.Kb3 Kc5 and White is in zugzwang.

45...fxe4 46.Ne3 Bc5 0-1.

Havana Defense
(1.d4 d5 2. Nf3 Bg4)

Actually, Black is just as likely to need this in the event of 1.Nf3 d5 2.d4.

Lobron–Hodgson
Haifa, 1989

1.Nf3 d5 2.d4 Bg4

We will adopt this rare line in combatting such openings as the Torre Attack and London Attack. It is the most forcing continuation against 2.Nf3.

3.Ne5

3.c4 gives Black the choice between adopting the Chigorin Defence (3...Nc6) or continuing in Queen's Gambit fashion. There is also the immediate capture to be considered. 3...Bxf3 4.gxf3 dxc4 5e4?! (5.e3 is evaluated by Cvetkovic and V. Sokolov (ECO II 1987) as better for White, but I am not convinced. 5...e5!? 6.dxe5 Qxd1+ 7.Kxd1 Nc6 8.f4 0-0-0+ 9.Bd2 f6 10.exf6 Nxf6 11.Bxc4 Bb4 12.Nc3 Bxc3 13.bxc3 Ne4 is just one example of Black's chances. I think the whole line needs practical tests.) e5! 6.dxe5 Qxd1+ 7.Kxd1 Nc6 8.f4 0-0-0+ 9.Bd2 Bc5 10.Rg1 Nge7 and Black was much better in Steinitz–Chigorin (m/9), Havana 1889.

3...	Bf5
4.g4	

4.c4 f6 (4...c6 is probably wiser. This position requires practical tests, but I do not see any serious problems for Black.) 5.Nf3 e6 6.Qb3! b6 7.Nc3 c6 8.a4 Na6 9.cxd5 exd5 10.e4! dxe4 11.Bxa6 exf3 12.0-0 ± Lasker–Schiffers, Nurnberg 1896.

| 4... | Bc8! |

Having provoked the weakness, the bishop returns home.

5.g5

5.e3 f6 6.Nd3 Nh6 7.h3 Nf7 8.f4 e5 9.fxe5 fxe5 10.dxe5 Qh4+ and Black has a strong attack.

| 5... | Bf5 |

Now that the pawn has advanced, Black returns to the outpost at f5.

6.c4	e6
7.Nc3	Ne7
8.Bg2	Nd7
9.cxd5	Nxd5

10.Nxd7

10.Nxd5 exd5 11.Bxd5 Nxe5 12.dxe5 Bb4+ 13.Kf1 Bh3+ 14.Kg1 c6
15.Bb3 Qc8 16.e3 Qf5 ∓

10...	**Qxd7**
11.e4	

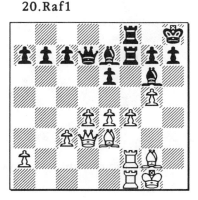

11...	Nxc3
12.bxc3	Bg6
13.0-0	Be7
14.Be3	0-0
15.f4	

Are the pawns strong or weak?

15...	f6!
16.h4	fxg5
17.hxg5	Kh8
18.Qd3	Rf7
19.Rf2	Raf8
20.Raf1	

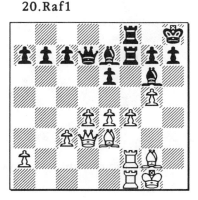

20...	h6
21.gxh6	gxh6
22.Kh1	Rg8
23.Rf3	Bh7
24.Rh3	Bf8
25.Bf3	Rf6

Black's position is solid enough. White has no real targets on the kingside.

26.Qd2	Rfg6
27.Rg1	Rxg1+
28.Bxg1	Qb5!
29.Qe1	Qd3
30.Bg2	Qc2

With just a queen, Hodgson has been able to infiltrate effectively.

31.Bf3	Qxa2
32.f5	exf5
33.exf5	Qf7
34.Bh2	Qxf5
35.Be5+	Bg7
36.Bxg7+	Rxg7
37.Bg2	

37.Qe8+ Rg8 38.Qe5+ Qxe5 39.dxe5 c6 40.Rxh6 Rg3 ∓

| 37... | Qg6 |
| 38.Bxb7? | |

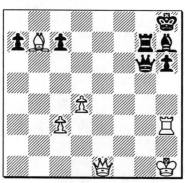

38...	c6
39.Qf2	Rxb7
40.Qf8+	Bg8

And White resigned, since the capture at h6 would still leave him a piece down. 0-1.

Other Queen Pawn Games

(1.d4 d5)

Veresov Attack

Alburt–Tal
USSR Ch, 1972

1.d4 Nf6 2.Nc3 d5

In our repertoire we will use the move order:

1.d4 d5 2.Nc3 Nf6 3.Bg5

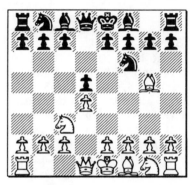

The Veresov Attack has never attracted many followers in the international arena, but it can be dangerous if one is not well prepared.

      3...   **Nbd7**
      4.f3

The most aggressive plan.

4.Nf3 b6 5.e3 (5.Ne5 Bb7 6.f4 Nxe5 7.fxe5 Ne4 8.Nxe4 dxe4 9.e3 Qd7 10.Bc4 e6 11.0-0 Bd5 12.Be2 b5 ∞.) Bb7 6.Ne5 Nxe5 7.dxe5 Ne4 8.Nxe4 dxe4 9.Qg4 Qd5! 10.Rd1 Qa5+ 11.c3 e6 12.Qf4 (12.Be2 h6 =.) Ba3!! 13.Be2 Bxb2 14.0-0 Bxc3 ∓ Tomson–Vasilshuk, Odessa 1960.

      4...   **c6**
      5.e4

5.Qd2 Qa5 6.e4 dxe4 7.Nxe4 Qxd2+ 8.Nxd2 b6 9.0-0-0 Bb7 10.Nc4 0-0-0 =. Fred–Wade, Moscow Olympiad 1956.

      5...   **dxe4**
      6.fxe4   **e5!**
      7.dxe5

7.Nf3 This is a move I prepared for the game. 7...exd4! A big TN! After the game in this note, Tal asked me why I chose the line, and was I familiar with his game against Alburt. I told him I was, but had an interesting idea in mind, but this move stopped me cold. (7...Qa5 was the old move, and here I was ready to employ an obscure idea. 8.Bxf6! Nxf6 9.Nxe5 Nxe4 10.Qf3! as in J.Brown–King, London 1978. But Ligterink's improvement at move 7 makes this moot.) 8.Nxd4 Bb4 White is now on the defensive and is hard-pressed to maintain the balance. My subsequent play is colored by the need to win for an IM norm. 9.Nf5 0-0 10.Bd3 Ne5 11.Bxf6 Qxf6 12.0-0 Bxf5 13.Rxf5 Qe7 Things don't look so bad, but there are serious problems at c3, d3, and e4. 14.Qe2 Bxc3 15.bxc3 Qc5+ 16.Kh1 Qxc3 17.Rb1 b5 ∓ 18.Rbf1 Rad8 19.Qf2 Rd7 20.h3 Nxd3 21.cxd3 Qxd3 22.e5 Qc4 23.Rg5 g6 24.Kh2 Re8 25.h4 h6 26.Qf5 Qxh4+ 27.Kg1 Qd4+ 0-1, Schiller–Ligterink, Reykjavik 1986. This loss cost me an IM norm, and I have not had success with the Veresov since.

7...	Qa5
8.exf6	

8.Bxf6 gxf6 9.e6 (9.exf6 Nxf6 10.Qd4 Bg7 11.0-0-0 0-0 ∓ 12.Qa4? Qxa4 13.Nxa4 Nxe4 14.Nh3 Bxh3 0-1, Philippe–Kennefick, Haifa Olympiad 1976.) fxe6 10.Bc4 (10.Qg4 Ne5 11.Qh5+ Ke7 12.0-0-0?? Nd3+-+) Bb4 11.Nge2 Ne5 and Black can be satisfied with the position. 12.Bb3 Rg8 13.a3 Bxc3+ 14.Nxc3 Rxg2 Now things get very exciting! 15.Qh5+ Rg6 16.Qh3! (16.Qxh7 Nf3+ 17.Kf2 Qg5!! 18.Kxf3 Rh6-+) Ng4 17.0-0-0! Nf2 18.Qxh7 Qg5+ 19.Kb1 Rg7 20.Qh8+ Rg8 21.Qh7 Rg7 22.Qh8+ Rg8 was agreed drawn in Rossetto–Gufeld, Camaguey 1974.

8...	Qxg5
9.fxg7	Bxg7
10.Qd2	

10.Nf3? Qe3+ 11.Be2 Bxc3+ 12.bxc3 Qxc3+ 13.Kf1 Nf6 ∓

10...	Qxd2+
11.Kxd2	Nc5
12.Bd3	Be6
13.Nf3	0-0-0
14.Ke2	b5
15.a3	a5
16.h3	Rhe8
17.Rhd1	

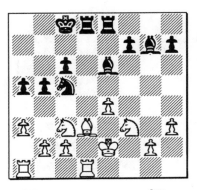

17...	f5!
18.e5	

18.exf5 Bxf5+ 19.Kf2 Bxd3 20.cxd3 Nxd3+ ∓

18...	Nd7
19.Re1	Bxe5
20.Kf2	Bf6
21.Re3	Nc5
22.Rae1	Kd7

Black's pieces are much more active and the bishop pair is a tangible asset. Now White self-destructs, tempted by a sacrificial line which is too easily declined.

23.Nxb5?	f4!
24.Re5	

24.R3e2 Nxd3+ 25.cxd3 cxb5

24...Nxd3+ 25.cxd3 cxb5 26.Rxb5 Rb8 27.Ne5+ Kd6 28.Rxa5 Bh4+ 0-1.

Colle System

Alekhine–Colle
San Remo, 1930

1.d4 Nf6 2.Nf3 d5 3.e3

Introducing the Colle System, which strikes irrational fear into the hearts of many amateurs even though it is considered completely harmless in serious play. It enters our repertoire via1.d4 d5 2.e3 Bf5 3.Nf3 Nf6.

3...	Bf5!

White wants to place a bishop at d3, so this move has psychological as well as practical effect.

4. Bd3

4.c4 e6 5.Qb3 Nc6 6.c5 (6.Qxb7 Nb4!) Qc8 7.Bb5 Nd7 8.Bxc6 bxc6 9.0-0 g6 10.Nbd2 Bg7 11.Nh4 Qa6! 12.Nxf5 exf5 13.Qc3 Nf6 14.Nb3 Ne4 and Black had the advantage in Colle–Nimzowitsch, Frankfurt 1930. Black's hypermodern treatment of the opening is highly instructive.

4.Nbd2 c6 5.Bd3 Bxd3 6.cxd3 e6 7.0-0 Be7 8.Re1 0-0 9.e4 White achieves his objective. So what? 9..Na6 10.e5 Nd7 11.Nf1 c5! 12.dxc5 Ndxc5 13.a3 Qd7 14.b4 Na4 and again Black is better, because without the light-squared bishop there is no hope of a kingside attack by White, Colle–Bogoliubow, San Remo 1930.

4...	e6
5.Bxf5	exf5

Although Black has weakened his pawn structure, he has achieved complete control of the light squares in the center.

6.0-0	Nbd7
7.c4	dxc4
8.Qa4	Bd6
9.Nbd2	0-0
10.Nxc4	Nb6
11.Nxb6	axb6
12.Qc2	Qd7
13.Ne5	Qe6
14.Nc4	Be7

Black must not allow this piece to be captured, as it is the source of much of his control of the dark-squares. The position illustrates the main weakness of the Colle—the bad bishop locked behind a chain of pawns.

15.Bd2	Rfd8
16.a4	Ne4

The idea is not to capture the bishop, but just to place the knight on a more effective square.

17.Rfd1	**f4!**

Black starts to crack open the kingside.

18.Be1	**fxe3**
19.Nxe3	

19.fxe3 Bg5

19...	**c6**
20.Nc4	**Ra6!**

The powerful rook becomes a babysitter, but this frees the rest of the forces to undertake more serious actions.

21.b4	**h6**

Just a defensive measure. Black's position is so strong that he can afford such luxuries.

22.Ra3	

22.Rac1 would have been more solid. After all, White is hardly going to be able to get a kingside attack rolling.

22...	**b5!**
23.axb5	

23.Na5?? Rxa5 24.bxa5 Bxa3

23...	**cxb5**
24.Rxa6	**bxa6**
25.Ne5	

25.Na5 would place the knight in a useless position.

25...	**Bf6!**

An effective exploitation of the pin on the d-file.

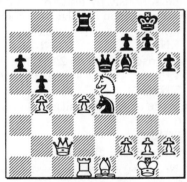

26.Qxe4	

26.Nf3 Ng5! 27.Nxg5 hxg5 28.Bc3 Bxd4! 29.Bxd4? Rxd4 30.Rxd4 Qe1+#

26...	**Bxe5**
27.f4?	

27.g3 Bxd4! 28.Rxd4 Rxd4 29.Qxd4 Qxe1+ was best, according to Alekhine, but even so Black is much better after the queen retreats to e6.

27...	**Bxd4+**
28.Rxd4	**Rxd4 0-1.**

Blackmar-Diemer Gambit

Sawyer–O'Connell
Correspondence, 1989

1.d4 d5 2.e4

The Blackmar-Diemer Gambit is the favorite of a fanatical bunch of amateurs but is not taken seriously by titled players. It is a lot of fun to play as White but there is no reason for Black to worry if well-prepared.

2...	**dxe4**
3.Nc3	**Nf6**

This position can also arise via 1.d4 d5 2.Nc3 Nf6 3.e4 dxe4.

4.f3	**exf3**
5.Nxf3	**e6**

The Euwe Defense is the strongest available, in my opinion.

6.Bg5	**Be7**
7.Bd3	

The standard move, though there are alternatives:

a) 7.Qd2 h6 8.Bh4 Nc6 9.0-0-0 Ne4! 10.Nxe4 Bxh4 11.g3 Be7 12.h4 Qd5 and White has less than nothing for the pawn.

b) 7.Bb5+ Bd7 8.Qe2 Nc6!? (8...a6 9.Bd3 0-0 10.0-0 Nc6 11.a3 h6 12.Bd2 Bd6 13.h3 gave White some compensation in Stummer–Kiesei, Correspondence 1958, and in my monograph on the Blackmar Diemer Gambit I suggested that this is the best path to follow for White. But now I think that the immediate knight move may be better.) 9.0-0-0 h6

b1) 10.Bd2 a6

b11) 11.Bxc6 Bxc6 12.Ne5 Nd7 13.Nxc6 bxc6 14.Qf3 Bf6 15.Qxc6 0-0 16.Bf4 e5 17.dxe5 Bxe5 18.Bxe5 (18.Rxd7 Bxf4+ 19.Kb1 Qg5 20.g3 Be5 ∞.) Nxe5 19.Rxd8 Nxc6 20.Rxf8+ Kxf8 21.Nd5 Rc8 22.Re1 Nd4 with the idea of Ne6 =.;

b12) 11.Bd3 Nb4 and again White is hard pressed to justify the investment of the pawn.;

b2) 10.Bh4 Nb4 11.Bxd7+ Nxd7 and White's attack has run out of steam.

7...	Nc6!

8.a3

8.0-0 Nxd4 9.Kh1 Nxf3 10.Qxf3 (Fechner–Schneider, Correspondence n.d.) 10...Bd7! with the idea of Bc6. 11.Qxb7 Rb8 12.Qxa7 Rxb2 and the extra pawn should suffice.

8.Qd2 h6 9.Be3 Nd5 10.Nxd5 (10.0-0-0 Nxe3 11.Qxe3 Bf6 ∓) exd5 11.c3 (Sawyer–Riley, USA 1989) 11...Bg4 12.Ne5 (12.0-0 Bxf3 13.Rxf3 Qd7 14.Qf2 Bf6 15.Re1 0-0-0 ∓) Nxe5 13.dxe5 Bh4+ 14.g3 Bg5 ∓∓

8...	h6!

9.Bd2

9.Bf4 g5 10.Be5 g4 11.Nh4 Rg8 ∓∓—Diemer.

9...	0-0

9...Nd5!? might be stronger.

10.0-0

10.Qe2 a6 11.0-0-0 b5 and Black's chances are no worse.

10...	Nxd4
11.Qe1	b6
12.Kh1	Bb7
13.Bxh6	Nxf3!
14.gxf3	Qd4!

Now Black will be able to use his queen on the kingside—for both attack and defense!

15.Be4	Nxe4
16.fxe4	f5!
17.Rg1	Rf7

Black has more than enough support for g7.

18.Rg2	fxe4 0-1.

English/Reti/Catalan

(1.c4 e6 2.Nf3 d5)

Flank openings are notorious for their transpositional jungles. To help clear a path, I have chosen a set of defenses which are based on the single idea of building a pawn chain with e6–d5–c6, developing a bishop at e7 and a knight at f6. In addition, most of the examples involve kingside castling and play on the queenside.

Naranja–Larsen
Bauang, 1973

1.c4 Nf6 2.g3 e6 3.Bg2 d5 4.Nf3

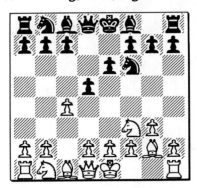

This position can be reached via many move orders.

4...	c6
5.Qc2	

5.d4 leads into the Catalan, which we will examine in another game.

5.0-0? dxc4 6.Ne5 Qd4 so it is not easy to get the pawn back.

5.b3 brings us definitively into the realm of the Reti. 5...a5 The thematic move, as we shall see below in our main line. 6.0-0 (6.Bb2 a4 7.Na3 Nbd7 8.0-0 Be7 9.d3 0-0 10.Nc2 Qb6 11.Bc3 Rd8 =. Sherwin–Fuster, Portoroz Interzonal 1958.) a4 7.bxa4 (7.Ba3 Bxa3 8.Nxa3 Qe7! 9.Qc1 0-0 10.Qb2 Nbd7 11.b4 e5! 12.Nh4 Rd8 =. Barcza–Bronstein, Hungary vs. USSR 1955.) dxc4 8.Qc2 Qa5 9.Qxc4 Qxa4 10.Qd3 Nbd7 11.Nc3 Qa5 12.Bb2 Be7 13.Ne4 0-0 14.Nxf6+ Nxf6 =. Geller–Bronstein, USSR 1964.

| 5... | a5!? |

Black's strategy involves Na6, but it is more conveninent to do so with the pawn at a5.

> **6.0-0**

6.b3 might be met by 6…a4.

6…	**Na6**
7.a3	**Be7**
8.d4	**0-0**
9.Nbd2	

9.Ne5 Nd7! 10.Nxd7 Bxd7 11.e4 dxc4 with the idea of b5, c5—Larsen.

9…	**b6**

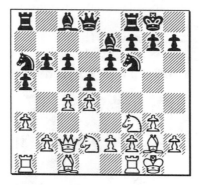

Black can claim equality here.

> **10.e4?!**

This is premature, since Black is prepared to increase the pressure on the light squares.

10…	**Bb7!**
11.exd5	**cxd5**

Now Black has the advantage, because White's center is vulnerable and his pieces are ineffective.

12.Ne5	**Qc7**
13.b3	**Bd6**
14.Bb2	**Rfd8!**

Even though the d-file seems crowded, it is important to keep the pressure on.

15.Rfe1	**Rac8**
16.Rad1	**Qe7!**

Black has plenty of targets to attack. Here White should have advanced the a-pawn but was perhaps overly concerned with the hole at b4. Still, the defense he actually chose gets him into big trouble.

17.Qc1?!	**dxc4**
18.bxc4	**Bxg2**

19.Kxg2

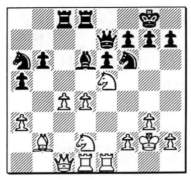

19...	b5!
20.c5	Bxe5
21.Rxe5	Qb7+!
22.Kg1	Nb8!

Time to bring the horse back into the game!

23.Rde1?!

It is not clear what the point of this move is.

23...	Nc6
24.Ne4	Ne8!
25.Rh5	

White lets the central pawn go in the hope of building a kingside attack, but there isn't the strength to make that work.

25...	Nxd4
26.Bxd4	Rxd4
27.Qb1	

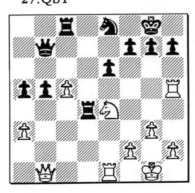

27...	Rxe4!

This leads to a winning position.

**28.Rxe4 Nf6 29.Reh4 Nxh5 30.Rxh5 f5 31.Qe1 Qd5-+ 32.g4 h6
33.Rh3 Rxc5 34.gxf5 exf5 35.Rc3 Rxc3 36.Qxc3 Qd1+ 37.Kg2
Qg4+ 38.Kf1 Qc4+ 39.Qxc4+ bxc4 40.Ke2 g5 41.Kd2 g4
42.Kc3 h5 43.Kxc4 a4 44.Kd5 Kf7 45.Ke5 Kg6 46.Kf4 Kf6
47.h3 gxh3 48.Kg3 Ke5 49.Kxh3 Kd4 50.Kh4 Kc3 0-1.**

Geller–Larsen
Copenhagen, 1966

1.c4 e6

We choose this reponse to the English, as it is the one most likely to lead to Queen's Gambit positions which are already part of our repertoire.

2.g3

2.Nc3 d5 pretty much forces 3.d4, as otherwise 3...d4 can be annoying.

2.Nf3 d5 3.g3 Nf6 4.Bg2 Be7 will transpose into the main line.

2...	d5
3.Bg2	Nf6
4.Nf3	Be7
5.0-0	0-0
6.d4	

We have now reached the main line of the Catalan.

6...   Nbd7

6...c6 can be played here, but the knight will go to d7 in any event.

7.Qc2

7.b3 can be played without a preliminary 7.Qc2. Play will usually transpose to the main lines. 7...c6 8.Bb2 b5!? 9.Nbd2 (9.c5 a5 should give Black sufficient counterplay.) b4!? As far as I know, this move, given in the 1987 edition of my Catalan book, has still not been tried, but I like the look of Black's position.

**7...   c6
8.b3**

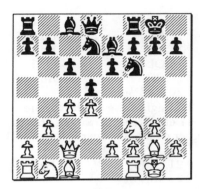

As with most flank games, this position can be reached by myriad move orders. But now we will adopt an aggressive, typically Larsenian approach.

8.Bf4 Nh5 9.Bd2 f5 =. O'Kelly–Bisguier, Caracas 1970.

8.Rd1 b5 9.c5 Ne4 10.a4 b4 11.Nbd2 f5 12.Ne1 Bf6 13.Nb3 a5 14.Nd3 ECO II (1991) claims a slight advantage for White here, based on Gheorghiu– Gobet, Biel 1983, but if there is one, it is difficult to see after 14...Ba6.

8...	b5!

I will accept Larsen's evaluation here, though ECO is not as impressed.

9.Nbd2

9.c5 Ne4 10.Bb2 f5. Strangely, this is not even mentioned in ECO II (1991)! 11.Ne1 Qe8!? 12.f3 Nef6 13.Nd3 a5! ∞. Van der Vliet–Bohm, Dutch Championship 1981.

9.Bf4!? bxc4 10.bxc4 Ba6 11.Nbd2 Qa5!? 12.e4 dxe4 13.Ng5 (13.Nxe4 Nxe4 14.Qxe4 Bxc4 15.Ng5 Nf6 ∓) h6 14.Ngxe4 Nxe4 15.Nxe4 e5 16.dxe5 Nxe5 ∞.

9...	bxc4!
10.bxc4	Ba6
11.Bb2	

11.Qa4 seems an obvious reply, but Black can respond with Qc8! and Nb6 is a real threat.

11...	Rb8
12.Rab1	Qa5!

Black has achieved equality.

13.Bc3	Bb4
14.Rxb4	Rxb4
15.Rc1!	

15.a3?? Qa4! and White's position is hopeless.

15...	Qa4
16.Bxb4	Qxb4
17.e3	Rc8
18.Qb3	Qa5
19.Bf1	h6
20.Rc3?!	

20.Qc3 Qa4 21.Qb3 might have led to a more peaceful conclusion. 21...Qa5! 22.Qc3 Qa4 etc. Now, however, the game becomes more interesting, in a manner which is more pleasant for Black.

20...	c5!
21.cxd5	Nxd5
22.Rc1	

22.Bxa6 allows the powerful zwischenzug Rb8!

22...	Bxf1
23.Nxf1	Rb8
24.Qc2	Nb4
25.Qd2	Qxa2
26.dxc5	Qxd2
27.N1xd2	

Black's endgame advantage is larger than might be revealed by a superficial examination of the position. It is not a matter of the outside passed pawn, which will play no important role. Rather it is the holes in White's kingside.

27...	Rc8
28.Ra1	Rc7
29.Nb3	e5
30.Ra4	Nd3
31.c6	Nb6
32.Ra1	Nc4
33.Ra4?	

Black fails to appreciate the danger. He should have defended the c-pawn with 33.Ra6, but the fact that Black has failed to swap pawns up to this point may have lulled Geller into a false sense of security.

| 33... | Rxc6! |
| 34.Rxa7 | |

34...	Rf6!
35.Rd7	

35.Kg2 e4

35...	Nxf2!
36.Kxf2	e4
37.Nbd4	Ne5!
38.Rd8+	Kh7
39.Re8	Nxf3
40.Ke2	

40.Nxf3 Rxf3+ 41.Ke2 f5 ∓

40.Kg2 Nd2! ∓

40...	Nxh2
41.Rxe4	Nf1
42.Rg4	g5!
43.Nb5	

43.Nf3? Rxf3! 44.Kxf3 Nh2+

43...Kg6 44.Nc3 h5 0-1.

Bird's Opening

(1.f4)

Antoshin–Panchenko
USSR, 1983

1.f4 e5

The From Gambit is our reply to the Bird's Opening. If 2.e4, then we transpose into the King's Gambit.

2.fxe5   d6
3.exd6

3.Nf3 Bg4!? 4.e4 dxe5 5.Bc4 Nd7 6.Nc3 Bc5 7.d3 Ngf6 8.Bg5 h6 9.Bh4 c6 10.h3 Bh5 11.Qe2 g5 12.Bf2 b5 and in Hayward–Nolan, Correspondence 1987, Black had an initiative on both sides of the board.

3...   Bxd6

This is a very complicated opening, and there is no room to squeeze in all of the details in a repertoire book, but I have written a monograph on the From, published in 1992 by Chess Enterprises.

4.Nf3   g5

5.g3

5.d4 g4 6.Ng5 (6.Ne5 Bxe5 7.dxe5 Qxd1+ 8.Kxd1 Nc6 9.Nc3 Be6! 10.Bf4 0-0-0+ 11.Ke1 Nge7 12.e3 Ng6 and in Chigorin–Tarrasch, Vienna 1898, Black had solved the problems of the opening. Dogmatic old Tarrasch—who would have thought of him on the Black side of this opening!) 6...f5 Black will win the knight, but White gets compensation. These are wild lines! 7.e4 h6 8.e5 Be7 9.Nh3 gxh3 10.Qh5+ Kf8 11.Bc4

Rh7! 12.Qg6 Rg7 13.Bxh6 Nxh6 If you want to play 13…Bb4+, you had better be prepared to study a lot of theory. This move is good enough for equality. 14.Qxh6 Bb4+ 15.c3 (15.Ke2 Qg5 returns to the complex line, though as a practical matter I think that 15.c3 is more likely in this move order. 16.Qxg5 Rxg5 17.g3! f4! 18.c3 Bg4+! 19.Ke1 fxg3 20.hxg3 Be7 21.Nd2 Nc6 22.Ne4 Rh5 23.Nf2 Nxe5! 24.dxe5 Rxe5+ 25.Kd2 Rd8+ 26.Kc2 Bf5+ 27.Kb3 b5! 28.Bf1 Rd2 ∓ Daudswards–Gulbis, Latvia 1988.) Qg5 16.Qxh3 Nc6 17.0-0 Nxe5! 18.dxe5 Bc5+ 19.Kh1 Ke7 20.b4 Be6! with the idea of Rh8. 21.Nd2 Rh8 22.Nf3! Qg6 23.Nh4 and now perhaps Black should settle for the draw by repeating the position. Instead, in Theiler–Ghitescu, Romania 1956, he tried for more and lost.

5…	g4
6.Nh4	Ne7
7.d4	

7.Bg2 Ng6 8.Nxg6 hxg6 9.0-0? Rxh2! 10.Kxh2 Qh4+ 11.Kg1 Bxg3 12.Rxf7 Qh2+ 13.Kf1 Kxf7 ∓ 14.d3 Nc6 15.Qd2 Kg7 16.Qc3+ Be5 17.Qc4 Be6!! 18.Qxe6 Rf8+ 19.Ke1 Qxg2 20.Qd7+ Kh8 21.Bh6 Qh1+ 0-1., Lazarevic–Basagic, Yugoslavia 1988.

7.e4 Ng6 8.Nf5 (8.Nxg6 hxg6 9.Bg2 Rxh2! 10.0-0 Bxg3 ∓ Jocobsen–Petersen, Danish Championship 1970.) Nc6 9.Bg2! Bxf5 10.exf5 Qe7+ 11.Qe2 Nd4! 12.Qxe7+ Nxe7 ∓

7…	Ng6
8.Nxg6	

8.Ng2 h5!? Not the most common move, but it seems good enough and avoids a lot of messy theory. 9.e4 h4 10.e5 Be7! 11.Rg1 Bf5 12.Be3 Nc6 13.c3 Qd7 14.Bb5 0-0-0 and Black had a promising position in Genser–Jonassen, Correspondence 1979.

8…	hxg6
9.Qd3	

9.Bg2? Rxh2 10.Rxh2 Bxg3+ 11.Kf1 Bxh2 ∓

9…	Nc6
10.c3	Qe7
11.Bg2	Bf5
12.e4	0-0-0
13.0-0?!	

13.Be3! Rde8! 14.Nd2 g5! 15.exf5 Qxe3+ 16.Qxe3 Rxe3+ 17.Kf2 Rhe8 18.Bd5 Ne7 19.Bxf7 Rf8 20.Be6+ Kd8 with a good game for Black in Langheld–Simchen, Correspondence 1990.

13…	Ne5!
14.Qd1	

14.Qe3 Bd7 15.Qg5 Nf3+ 16.Bxf3 f6 is unclear, according to Panchenko.

14…	Nf3+

15.Bxf3   gxf3
16.exf5

16...Rxh2!! 17.Qxf3 Rh3 18.Bf4 Bxf4 19.Qxf4 Rdh8 20.Qf3
Qg5 21.Kf2 Rh2+ 22.Kg1 Rh1+ 0-1.

Nimzowitsch–Larsen Attack

(1.b3)

Larsen–Spassky
USSR vs. Rest of World , 1970

1.b3 e5!

When White "forgets" to play 1.Nf3 before turning his attention to the other flank, then Black should take advantage of this lapse.

2.Bb2	**Nc6**
3.c4	

3.e3 d5 4.Bb5 Bd6 is a reversed Owen's Defense, which should not cause Black to lose any sleep. 5.f4!? Qe7 6.Nf3 f6!? 7.Nc3 Be6 8.f5!? Bf7! is fine for Black.

3...	**Nf6**
4.Nf3?!	

Larsen plays his typical fighting chess in this important encounter, but this is just reckless.

4.e3 d6 leads to a reversed Closed Sicilian in which White has adopted a very artificial formation. Black could also play 4...d5, but then I think that the recklessness is perhaps on the other foot!

4...	**e4**
5.Nd4	**Bc5**
6.Nxc6	

6.e3 Bxd4 7.exd4 d5 8.cxd5 Qxd5 is just awful for White.

6.Nc2 d5 7.cxd5 Qxd5 is acceptable for Black since 8.Bxf6 gxf6 9.Nc3 Qf5 10.Ne3 (10.e3 Ne5!) Bxe3 11.dxe3 Be6 12.g3 h5 13.h4 Qe5 is not much fun for White!

6...	**dxc6!**

The normal instinct would lead to a capture with the other pawn, but Spassky understands that the pressure on the d-file is more valuable.

7.e3

7.d4 exd3 8.Qxd3 Qxd3 9.exd3 Bf5 10.d4 Bxb1 11.Rxb1 Bb4+ 12.Kd1 0-0-0 gives Black a clear advantage.

7...	**Bf5**
8.Qc2	**Qe7**
9.Be2	

9.d4 exd3 10.Bxd3 Bxd3 11.Qxd3 Rd8 12.Qc2 0-0 13.0-0 Ne4 and Black has considerable pressure.

9...	**0-0-0**

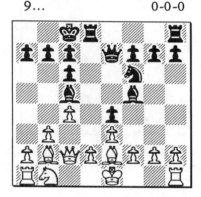

The general concensus was that White had to capture at f6 here. Instead, Larsen creates a fatal weakness in his position.

10.f4?

10.Bxf6 Qxf6 11.Nc3 Qe5 12.0-0 Bd6 13.g3 h5 with a strong attack for Black.

10...	**Ng4**
11.g3	

11.Bxg4 Bxg4 12.h3 Qh4+ ∓

11...	**h5**
12.h3	**h4!!**
13.hxg4	

13.Bxg4 Bxg4 14.hxg4 hxg3 15.Rg1 (15.Rxh8 Rxh8 is an exchange of a defender (at h1) for a spectator (at d8), which obviously works to Black's advantage.) Rh1!! 16.Rxh1 g2 17.Rg1 Qh4+ 18.Ke2 Qxg4+ 19.Ke1 Qg3+ 20.Ke2 Qf3+ 21.Ke1 Be7!! A monster move which forces mate.

13...	**hxg3**
14.Rg1	

14...	**Rh1!!**

The brilliant theme works anyway!

15.Rxh1	g2
16.Rf1	

16.Rg1 Qh4+ 17.Kd1 Qh1! 18.Qc3 Qxg1+ 19.Kc2 Qf2 20.gxf5 Qxe2 21.Na3 Bb4!! was demonstrated by Spassky after the game. For those who miss the point: 22.Qxb4 Qd3+ 23.Kc1 g1R+#

16...	Qh4+
17.Kd1	gxf1Q+

and Larsen resigned, as there was no way even to get past move 20.

18.Bxf1	Bxg4+
19.Be2	

19.Kc1 Qe1+ 20.Qd1 Qxd1+

19...	Qh1+# 0-1

Reversed Modern

(1.g3)

Lobron–Korchnoi
Bad Kissingen, 1981

1.g3

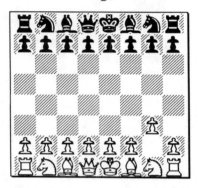

OK, this really isn't a horrible move, and usually leads to a reversed Modern Defense. But since part of the job here is to build the reader's confidence…

1…	e5
2.Bg2	d5
3.d3	g6
4.c4	

This is a particularly aggressive option, the kind of thing that sometimes scares people. Look at all that pressure on the light squares. My advice: Don't worry, Be happy!

4…	d4
5.Nf3	

It would not make much sense to develop the knight at h3 in this formation.

5…	Nc6
6.0-0	Bg7

Since Black has not advanced his c-pawn, and has supported his center well, the Hypermodern goals which underly White's opening strategy have little hope of being fulfilled.

7.Nbd2	a5!

A useful move which restrains White's queenside, his only sphere of influence in this position.

8.Rb1	Nf6
9.b3	0-0

Black must hurry before White establishes a powerful bishop at a3.

10.a3	Qe7

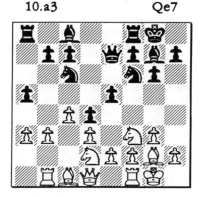

11.b4?

White is counting on the overloaded knight at c6, which must keep an eye on both b4 and e5. But there is a flaw in this grand design.

11...	axb4
12.axb4	Nxb4!
13.Nxe5	Na2

Yes, the future Grandmaster failed to recognize the danger at c3! Not all that surprising, really, since in the previous diagram the knight stood at c6, from which it is a long journey to c3. 0-1.

Sokolsky

(1.b4)

Lalic–Uhlmann
Sarajevo, 1980

1.b4 d5 2.Bb2 Qd6!?

Why not? The queen supports the center and attack the pawn. White is not likely to be well prepared for this line!

3.a3

3.b5 e5! (3...Qb4 4.Bc3 Qxb5 5.e4 Qd7 6.exd5 Qxd5 7.Nf3 and White has some play for the pawn.) 4.e3 Nf6 5.Nf3 Bg4 6.Be2 e4 7.Nd4 Bxe2 8.Qxe2 Nbd7 ∞.

3...	e5
4.e3	Nf6
5.d3	

This is designed to discourage any further advance of the e-pawn.
5.Nf3 Bg4 6.Be2 Nbd7 7.h3 Bh5 =.

5...	Nbd7
6.Nf3	c6
7.Be2	g6
8.c4	Bg7

Black has achieved a comfortable position, with the bishops opposed on the long diagonal.

9.cxd5	cxd5
10.0-0	0-0
11.Nc3	a6

12.Rc1	b6
13.Qc2	Bb7
14.h3	

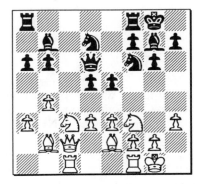

The stage is set for the middlegame. Black could just reposition a rook here, but he chooses to undertake active operations instead.

14...	d4
15.Nd1	

15.exd4 exd4 16.Nd1 Rac8 ∓

15...	Rac8
16.Qb1	Nd5
17.Re1	

17.e4 Nf4 18.Re1 f5 and White's position is cracked.

17...	dxe3
18.fxe3	b5!

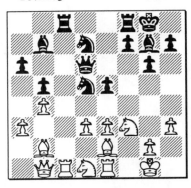

Now just look at the weak pawns at d3 and e3, ripe for the plucking!

19.Bf1	N7b6
20.Nd2	Na4

21.Qa1

21.Ba1 Rxc1 22.Qxc1 Rc8 23.Qb1 Nac3 24.Nxc3 Nxc3 25.Bxc3 Rxc3
26.Qb2 Qc6 with an overwhelming position.

21...	f5
22.Nb3	Rfe8
23.Na5	Ba8
24.Nc3	Nxb2
25.Qxb2	e4
26.d4	

Forced, but now the holes in White's position are permanent. The
bright side is that he doesn't live long enough to suffer much.

| 26... | Nxe3! |
| 27.Ne2 | |

27.Rxe3 Bxd4

27...f4 28.Rxc8 Rxc8 29.Rc1 Rf8

The d4-square cannot be maintained. 0-1.

The "Macho" Grob

(1.g4)

Duckworth–Schiller
San Diego, 1988

1.g4 d5 2.h3 c6 3.Bg2 e5

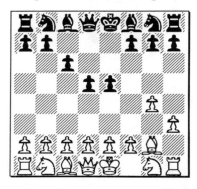

It is generally considered best to counter a flank action with activity in the center of the board. Building a strong center is therefore a good idea.

4.d3

4.d4 e4 5.c4 Bd6 6.Nc3 Ne7 is a very solid position for Black. 7.Bg5! (7.g5?! Be6 8.h4 Nf5 9.Bh3 0-0 10.cxd5 cxd5 11.Nxd5 Ng3! puts White in deep trouble. 12.Nf6+ gxf6 13.fxg3 Bxg3+ 14.Kf1 Nc6 15.Be3 Nb4 16.Kg2 Nd5! 17.Kxg3 Nxe3 18.Qd2 Qd6+ 19.Kf2 Qf4+ 20.Nf3 exf3 and in Basman–Keene, Manchester 1981, White resigned. I spoke to Basman just after the game and he was pessimistic about the Grob, though his confidence returned quickly, as usual! Basman–Singh, Lloyds Bank London, 1989 saw instead 7.Qb3 0-0 8.Bd2 Na6 9.Rc1 Bb4 10.Nxe4 dxe4 11.Bxb4 c5 12.Bxc5 Nxc5 13.dxc5 f5 14.gxf5 Bxf5 15.h4 Ng6 16.Qc3 Nf4 17.Bf1 Qc7 18.h5 Rad8 19.h6 Nd3+ 20.exd3 exd3 21.Nf3 Rde8+ 22.Kd1 Bg4 23.Bxd3 Rxf3 24.Kc2 Bf5 25.Rcd1 Rd8 26.Rhg1 g6 27.Bxf5 Rxc3+ 28.bxc3 Rxd1 29.Be6+ Kf8 30.Rxd1 Qxc5 31.Rd4 Qe5 32.Bg4 Qg5 33.f3 Qxh6 34.Rd8+ Ke7 35.Rd7+ Kf6 36.Rxb7 Qh2+ 37.Kb3 h5 38.Bd7 Qf2 39.Rb5 Qxf3 40.Kb4 Qd1 41.Rd5 Qb1+ 42.Kc5 0-1. and again Basman was let down by his pet line) 7...f6 8.Bd2 0-0 9.Qb3 Kh8 10.Rc1 Na6 with unclear complications in Basman–Kudrin, Manchester 1981.

4...   Bd6

Benjamin and I suggest 4...Ne7 in our book, but I find this move a bit more active.

5.Nc3	Ne7
6.e4	Be6

6...d4 7.Nce2 would have played into White's hands, as f2–f4 would be possible.

7.Nf3	Nd7
8.0-0	f6

Black's position looks a bit artificial, but it is actually very well balanced and does not have any weaknesses.

9.d4	0-0
10.dxe5	Nxe5
11.exd5	cxd5!

The pawn is secure and does not represent a weakness. The semi-open c-file is now available to Black.

12.Nd4	Bf7
13.b3	Rc8
14.Bb2	Bb4
15.Nce2	Qd7
16.a3	Ba5
17.f4?	

White clearly fails to appreciate the vulnerability of his kingside, a malady which afflicts many practicioners of the "macho" Grob.

17...	N5g6
18.f5	Ne5
19.Nf4	Bb6
20.Kh1	Bxd4!
21.Bxd4	N7c6
22.Rf2	Rfe8
23.Qd2	Qd6!

With the dark-squared bishop gone, the queen takes over the role of guardian of the relevant squares.

24.Bb2	d4!
25.Rd1	Rcd8
26.Nd3	Bd5
27.Qf4?	Nxd3
28.Rxd3	Qxf4
29.Rxf4	Re1+
30.Kh2	Re2

The pin is excruciating.

31.Rg3	Rxc2
32.Ba1	

32.Bxd4 Bxg2

32...	d3
33.g5	Bxg2
34.gxf6	

34.Rxg2 Rxg2+ 35.Kxg2 fxg5 36.Rg4 d2

34...	Bd5+
35.Kg1	Rc1+
36.Kf2	Rxa1

White should have resigned here, but it was "Action" chess.

37.Rxg7+	Kh8
38.Ke3	

38.Rh4 Bg8 39.Rxb7 d2-+

38...Ne5 39.Rf2 Re1+ 40.Kf4 Re2 41.Rf1 Nf7 42.Rd1 Bxb3 43.Rdg1 d2 44.Kg4 d1Q 45.Kh5 Rg2+ 46.Rg4 Rxg4 47.Rxg4 Rg8 48.Kh4 Rxg4+ 49.hxg4 Qg1 50.a4 Qh2+ 0-1.

Saragossa Opening

(1.c3)

Rogers–Mortazavi
. British Championship, 1988
1.c3

An innocuous move. Almost any reply is good, but a Dutch strategy is a very effective choice, since c2–c3 is not part of White's better plans.

1...	f5

Now White cannot get in e2–e4.

2.d4

2.e4 fxe4 3.Qh5+ g6 4.Qe5 Nf6∓

2...	e6
3.g3	Nf6
4.Bg2	d5

Without a pawn at c4, White has no useful plan.

5.Nh3	Bd6
6.Bf4	0-0
7.Nd2	

7.Bxd6 Qxd6 8.Nf4 c5 9.0-0 Nc6 and ...e5 is coming soon.

7...	Qe7
8.Nf3	Ne4
9.Bxd6	cxd6!

Black now has more than enough support for an eventual e6–e5.

10.0-0	Nd7
11.Ne1	b5!

This secures the c4 square.

12.f3	Nef6
13.Nf2	

White tries to achieve the e4 break, but Black is well-developed.

13...	Bb7
14.Qd3	Nb6
15.Nc2	

15.e4 dxe4 16.fxe4 fxe4 17.Nxe4 Nxe4 18.Bxe4 Rxf1+ 19.Kxf1 Rf8+ 20.Kg2 Qf7! 21.Bxb7 Qxb7+ 22.Nf3 e5 23.dxe5 dxe5 24.Re1 Nc4 25.b3 Nd2! 26.Re3 e4 27.Qxd2 exf3+ 28.Kf2 Qf7 Δ Qh5.

15...	Rac8
16.Rfe1	Qf7!?

Black sacrifices an irrelevant pawn to deflect the enemy queen.

17.Qxb5	Nc4!

18.Qb3	f4
19.gxf4	

19.g4 would obviously render the Bg2 powerless.

19...	Rb8!
20.Nb4	a5
21.Nbd3	

The White queen has an escape path.

21...	Ne3

Not!

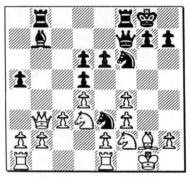

22.Nd1	Bc6
23.Nxe3	Rxb3
24.axb3	Nh5
25.Rxa5	Nxf4
26.Nxf4	Qxf4
27.Nf1	

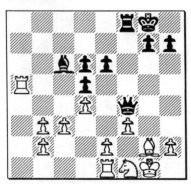

The useless White pieces are no match for the queen, despite the limited scope of Black's bishop.

27...	e5!

28.e3	Qg5
29.Kh1	

29.dxe5 d4!

29...	Qg6
30.Ra6	Qe8
31.Ng3	Qd7
32.Rea1	Kh8

Black plays this to avoid tricks on d5, e.g., 32...h6 33.R1a5 Rb8 34.dxe5 dxe5 35.f4 Rxb3?? 36.Rxc6 Qxc6 37.Bxd5+

33.f4	exf4
34.exf4	Bb5
35.Ra7	Qg4

All of the Black pieces are now active.

36.f5	h5
37.f6	

Desperation.

37...	gxf6
38.Rb7	Bd3
39.Rg1	h4
40.Nf1	Rg8

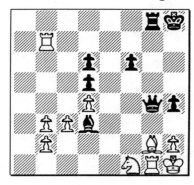

0-1

Anderssen's Opening

(1.a3)

Mieses–Cohn
Ostende, 1907

1.a3

A waiting move, usually played to induce a reversed Sicilian. It is not a bad move, but contributes little to White's game.

1.a4 is a bad move. Even Hugh Myers calls it dubious. 1...d5 2.Nf3 Nf6 and Black should just continue with a Queen's Gambit formation since a2–a4 is absolutely irrelevant there.

1...	d5
2.d4	Nf6

Again, Black should just ignore White's flank move, keeping in mind only that the b4 square will not be available.

3.e3	Bf5
4.Bd3	Bg6
5.Nc3	

5.c3 Nc6 6.Nf3 (6.f4 Be4!) Qd6 with the idea of e5.

5...	e6
6.Nf3	c5
7.Qe2	Nc6
8.0-0	Be7
9.dxc5	Bxc5

Black has wisely continued with development and has a comfortable game with greater control of the center.

10.e4	0-0
11.b4	

White has suddenly become aggressive, but two can play at that game!

11...	Nd4!
12.Qe1	dxe4
13.Nxe4	Nxf3+
14.gxf3	Bd4 ∓
15.Rb1	Nd5
16.Be3	e5!
17.Rd1	

17.Bxd4 exd4 would leave the dark squares too weak.

17...	Qh4
18.Kh1	Bh5
19.Be2	Rac8

White's weaknesses are easy to target.

20.Bxd4

20.c4 Bxe3 21.cxd5 Bf4 22.Ng3 Rc2 with the idea of Rfc8.

20...exd4 21.Rxd4 Nf4 22.Ng3 Nxe2 23.Qxe2 Qxd4 24.Nxh5 Rfe8 25.Qb5 Qe5 26.Qxe5 Rxe5 27.Nf4 Rf5 28.Ne2 Rxf3-+ 29.c3 a6 30.Rd1 Rxf2 0-1.

Drunken Knight Openings

(1.Nh3, 1.Na3, 1.Nc3)

Flugrath–Ter
Braake Correspondence, 1990
1.Nh3

The Amar, an absolutely mad and ridiculous opening.

1.Na3 The Durkin, or Sodium Attack. It is easy to meet. 1...d5 2.c4 c6 3.e3 e5 4.d4 exd4 5.exd4 Nf6 6.Bg5 Be7 7.Nf3 0-0 is one example of easy equality.

1.Nc3 is a very flexible move. 1...e5 Now 2.e4 transposes to the Vienna Game, which is already in our repertoire. Various other moves are possible, but Black can just continue sensibly. For example: 2.Nf3 Nc6 3.d4 exd4 4.Nxd4 Bb4 5.Nxc6 bxc6 =.

1...	d5
2.g3	e5
3.f4	

This is the Paris Gambit, a romantic but unprincipled move.

3.Bg2 f5 is perfectly playable for Black, though White, who is adopting a Modern setup with colors reversed, does not have a terrible position. Black should continue with piece development and central fortification with c7–c6.

3...	Bxh3
4.Bxh3	exf4
5.d4	

5.0-0 fxg3 6.hxg3 (6.e4 d4! 7.Qh5 Nf6 8.Qb5+ Nbd7 9.Qxb7 gxh2+ 10.Kxh2 Bd6+ and Black will castle and then go king-hunting.) Nf6 7.d3 Nc6 8.Nc3 (Tartakower–Lilienthal, 1933) 8...Be7! 9.Bf4 (9.Bg5 h6 10.Bf4 d4) d4 ∓ Benjamin & Schiller (1987).

5...	Bd6!
6.Rg1	

6.gxf4? Qh4+

6...	fxg3
7.hxg3	c6

Black already has the advantage, and can now simply develop and then exploit the weaknesses of White's pawn structure later.

8.Qd3	Qe7
9.Nd2	Nf6
10.Nf3	

White is forced to abandon his dream of e2–e4.

10...	**Nbd7**
11.Bd2	**Nh5**
12.g4	

What else?

12...	**Ng3**
13.0-0-0	

White is prepared to give up the e-pawn to release the pressure, but Black is more ambitious than that!

13...	**Ne4!**
14.c4??	

14.Be1 Bf4+ 15.Kb1 c5! 16.dxc5 Ndxc5 17.Qxd5 0-0! and a queenside attack is coming.

14.Be3 was probably best. Even so, White would have to face an onslaught on the queenside, perhaps with a straightforward pawn storm.

14...Nf2 15.Qb3 Nxh3 0-1.

Van't Kruy's Opening

(1.e3)

Mason–Winawer
Berlin, 1881

1.e3 b6

This is a logical reply to 1.b3, since White is indicating a preference to play on the dark squares.

2.b3	**Bb7**
3.Bb2	**d6**

Black will contest the dark squares by establishing a pawn at e5. The slight weakening of the light squares in the center is not very important, as White cannot take advantage of them.

4.d4

4.f4 Nd7 5.Nf3 c5 6.Be2 Qc7 7.0-0 e5 =.

4...	**Nf6**
5.Nf3	**Nbd7**
6.c4	**e5**

Black can be well satisfied with his opening play. He has established a stake in the center and is developing his forces smoothly.

7.Be2	**e4**
8.Nfd2	**c6**
9.Nc3	**d5**

Black has played the opening with apparent ease. The pressure against his pawn chain is not significant.

10.cxd5	**cxd5**

11.Rc1	**a6!**

A useful prophylactic move. The c-file can be contested later.

12.0-0	**Bd6**

The weakness of the kingside creates inviting targets for Black's forces. It will be very difficult for White to defend his monarch, an therefore the king should have remained in the center.

13.f3	**exf3**
14.Bxf3	**0-0**
15.e4	

White is playing programmatically, advancing in the center without taking into consideration the overall weakness of his position, especially the king.

15...	**dxe4**
16.Ndxe4	**Nxe4**
17.Nxe4?!	

17.Bxe4 Bxe4 18.Nxe4 Bxh2+ 19.Kxh2 Qh4+ 20.Kg1 Qxe4 and White does not have sufficient compensation for his pawn.

17...	**Bxe4**
18.Bxe4	**Qh4!**

Since the bishop at d6 is not under attack from a White knight, this move is even more powerful than the transposition into the previous variation which could have been effected by 18...Bxh2+.

19.Re1 Bxh2+ 20.Kf1 Rae8 21.Qf3 Bg3! 22.Re3 Bf4 23.Rce1

23.Rec3 Bxc1 24.Rxc1 Rxe4

23...Bxe3 24.Rxe3 Nf6 25.Bc6 Ng4! 26.Bxe8 Nh2+ 27.Kg1 Nxf3+ 28.gxf3 Qg3+ 29.Kf1 Qh3+ 0-1.

Clemenz Opening

(1.h3)

Mead–Morphy
New York, 1857

1.h3

This is a rather silly move, as the great Paul Morphy demonstrates.

1...	e5
2.e4	Nf6
3.Nc3	Bc5
4.Bc4	

So far we have a reversed Italian Game, where the move h2–h3 performs some small useful function keeping pieces out of g4. But in the Evans Gambit, that is not a key part of the strategy, so Morphy jumps right in.

4...	b5!?
5.Bxb5	c6
6.Ba4	0-0
7.Nge2	

7.Nf3 would have been better.

7...	d5
8.exd5	cxd5
9.d4	

9.d3 Qa5 10.a3 was suggested by Maroczy.

9...	exd4
10.Nxd4	Qb6
11.Nce2	Ba6

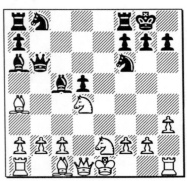

The Black bishops already exert considerable pressure.

12.c3	Bxe2
13.Kxe2	

13.Qxe2 Bxd4 14.cxd4 Qb4+ 15.Bd2 Qxa4.

13.Nxe2 Bxf2+ 14.Kf1 Na6—Maroczy.

13...	Bxd4
14.Qxd4	Qa6+
15.Kf3	Rc8
16.b3	Ne4
17.Bb2	

17.Qxd5 Nxc3 18.Qxa8 Qe2+ 19.Kf4 g5+ 20.Kxg5 Rc5+ 21.Kf4 Qxf2+ 22.Qf3 Ne2+ 23.Ke4 (23.Kg4 h5+) Qd4+.

17...	Nc6
18.Bxc6	Rxc6
19.Ke3	

19.Qxd5 Rf6+ 20.Kg4 (20.Kxe4 Re8+ 21.Kd4 Rf4+ 22.Kc5 Qb6+) Qe2+ 21.f3 Qxg2+ 22.Kh4 Qg3+ 23.Kh5 Rh6+.

19...Re8 20.Rhe1 Nxc3+ 21.Kf3 Rf6+ 22.Kg3 Qd6+ 23.f4 Ne2+ 24.Rxe2 Rxe2 25.Rf1 Rg6+ 26.Kf3 Rgxg2 0-1.

Index of Games

Index of Variations

NOTES

NOTES

NOTES

NOTES

NOTES

NOTES

NOTES